- Here And Now

Edited by Heather Killingray

First published in Great Britain in 2005 by:
Young Writers
Remus House
Coltsfoot Drive
Peterborough
PE2 9JX
Telephone: 01733 890066
Website: www.youngwriters.co.uk

SB ISBN 1 84602 189 8

Foreword

Young Writers was established in 1991 and has been passionately devoted to the promotion of reading and writing in children and young adults ever since. The quest continues today. Young Writers remains as committed to the fostering of burgeoning poetic and literary talent as ever.

This year's Young Writers competition has proven as vibrant and dynamic as ever and we are delighted to present a showcase of the best poetry from across the UK. Each poem has been carefully selected from a wealth of *Playground Poets* entries before ultimately being published in this, our thirteenth primary school poetry series.

Once again, we have been supremely impressed by the overall high quality of the entries we have received. The imagination, energy and creativity which has gone into each young writer's entry made choosing the best poems a challenging and often difficult but ultimately hugely rewarding task - the general high standard of the work submitted amply vindicating this opportunity to bring their poetry to a larger appreciative audience.

We sincerely hope you are pleased with our final selection and that you will enjoy *Playground Poets - Here And Now* for many years to come.

Contents

St John's CE Primary School, Worksop

The Poems

My Grandma

My grandma is the best
She's better than all the rest
She copes with it all and I
Can't say she's very tall

I turn to her when I'm scared or in trouble
And she always gives me a great big cuddle

You might not think that my grandma is so strong and brave
But you're wrong I'm afraid

She's my one and only grandma and I love her to bits
I wouldn't trade her for anything

As I have already told you she's the best
No one can put it to the test.

Hannah Taylor (11)

Darkness

Darkness is spicy
Darkness is icy
It sounds like the thumping of your heart

Darkness smells like smoke
It could make you choke
Darkness is a void as black as the night.

Joanne Harper-Hill (10)

Daisy's Seasons

Autumn poem

The cows graze quietly in the fields
While the sheep give birth for the very first time
And the farmer cuts his wheat

Winter poem

The field is covered with blustering snow
And the geese are flying south for the winter
The trees are full of icicles and snow

Summer poem

In the summer I play on my tree house
I camp under the stars at night
And swim in the swimming pool

Spring poem

The flowers start to grow
And the leaves peep from their buds
The birds eat lots and lots of berries.

Daisy Newton (7)

The World

The world is such a wonderful place
Full of different people from the human race
Spread out throughout the lands
Across the seas, mountains and sands

In many ways people are not the same
Some poor, some rich, some known for their fame
So many languages and colours around
Makes the world a mixture of sound.

Erin Macdonald Offer (10)
Airidhantuim Primary School, Shader, Isle of Lewis

Racism

The boy called me a name
Because my skin colour isn't the same
Hurt and upset I walk home
No friends, I am all alone

He doesn't know me
So how can it be
The hate in his eyes
Did he realise?

It is hard to understand
We both come from the same land
What did I do?
I am the same as you

He gave me a frown
Because my skin is brown
It makes me sad to see
But friends I'd like to be.

Conner MacDonald (11)
Airidhantuim Primary School, Shader, Isle of Lewis

The Night Sky

The night sky is a beautiful sight
The stars and the moon are so very bright
All of a sudden a star shoots past
It speeds through the sky incredibly fast

I have never seen a comet before
But I will keep looking forever more
To search for what magic I will see
Displayed in the darkness above me

I wonder when I look up at the night sky
Who and what is up there, so high?
If they're looking down, what can they see?
What I really wonder, is if they can see me?

Lauren MacDonald (10)
Airidhantuim Primary School, Shader, Isle of Lewis

Night

In the middle of the night
It is not very bright
I need a light to say
Goodnight
In the middle of the night

In the middle of the night
I dream of a fight
Then I wake James
And have a pillow fight
In the middle of the night

In the middle of the night
You might need a torch
If the moon is not bright
It is dark and spooky and scary and creepy
In the middle of the night.

Ian MacDonald (9)
Airidhantuim Primary School, Shader, Isle of Lewis

Night

At night it is not bright
I need a torch to go outside
I see a shadow
I get a fright
It was just a cat
On the doormat

I am shining my torch
High and low
I see a bat
Being chased by the cat

I keep watching the cat
As he prowls around
He jumps on the wall
Because a rat he has found.

Beth Macleod (7)
Airidhantuim Primary School, Shader, Isle of Lewis

Colours

Red is for danger
Red is a warning
Red is angry
Moods forming

Blue is for the sea
Blue is a sky
Blue is the winning team
In the match tie

White is for snow
White is a dove
White is the winter
On the land above

Green is for go
Green is a land
Green is a snake
Slithering on sand

Yellow is for the sun
Yellow is a melon
Yellow is a freshly
Squeezed lemon.

Jonathan Macleay (11)
Airidhantuim Primary School, Shader, Isle of Lewis

My Pet Dog

Don's black and white coat is lovely and soft
His big pointed ears droop down
He barks and squeals all night long
What a racket he makes all around

Don is a collie that rounds up sheep
He gets them all in the pen
Running and panting as he works
Doing the job so well.

Johanna MacDonald (8)
Airidhantuim Primary School, Shader, Isle of Lewis

The Night Race

The cars pull up at the red light
With their headlamps beaming bright
It changes to amber with revs at full
Hands at the ready, with a gearstick to pull
It turns to green and the racers go
Who will win, no one can know
The cars come up to the first turn
Will the driver in front ever learn?
The leading driver has lost his place
Will he ever get back in the race?
Here they come to the long straight
Which racer will now meet their fate?
Now the racers use their nitro's boost
For the driver in front's wheel nuts are coming loose!
The wheel comes off and the brake disk starts to grind
So the driver pulls over, raging blind
Now in their sight, the finishing line
They then zoom by with blinding body shine
The winner has now been given his pay
So he gets into his car and drives away

Andrew Taylor (11)
Airidhantuim Primary School, Shader, Isle of Lewis

A Scary Dream

A larming witches flying past

S keletons falling out of cupboards aghast
C an this be true? Is it real?
A fraid is how I feel!
R un, run as fast as you can
Y ou can't catch me, you evil tin man

D etermined to get out of his place
R unning I feel that I am in a life's race
E eek! Something is touching me
A ahh! What sort of monstrosity?
M um, mum, please save me!

Kerry Coleman (10)
Airidhantuim Primary School, Shader, Isle of Lewis

Swimming

As my name is called I walk nervously out
And wave to my friends and family

The hooter goes and I jump into the water
The butterflies in my tummy increasing their momentum

Taking hold of the wall, I go through my technique
Eager for the race to start

In these long moments I remember my journey
All the hard work at practice, the hours of pain

My thoughts turned to the coach who showed confidence in me
His dedication in training day after day

Blahh! Goes the hooter and off I go
Propelling through the water at breakneck speed

Watching the roof go rapidly by, in backstroke motion
Hoping to prove I can be the best

Excelling myself for my team, doing it all for them
My adrenalin pumping, my arms and legs streaking to home

I hit the wall and I have won
Another step to my goal, Olympics here I come

A girl is allowed to dream.

Kathryn Offer (12)
Airidhantuim Primary School, Shader, Isle of Lewis

My Cat Ealasaid

My cat Ealasaid is as black as night
Except her eyes which shine like a light
Sometimes she can be a bit of a pest
But I think she is still one of the best

She tries to catch birds as she dashes along
She thinks she can fly but she is so wrong
Her fur is so silky and soft as a feather
She likes nothing better than to roll in the heather.

Kayleigh Smith (8)
Airidhantuim Primary School, Shader, Isle of Lewis

War

War is the cry on all lips
It's a word I don't understand
All I know is things have changed
And my father is off to a faraway land

Sirens can be heard all around
My mother is in a frightful state
Getting me ready to flee the house
Trying to ensure we won't be too late!

A strange atmosphere can be felt
While in safety underground
People try to do their best
Amidst the bombing, exploding sound

We all sit side by side
Blankets and pillows can be found
Someone sings a cheery song
Despite the gloom, follows a merry sound

And as daylight comes, relief I feel
But still the uncertainty of the mess above
Nervously I emerge from the shelter
Hurt and devastation, no peace and love

And so the days and months become years
Suddenly, I hear a knock at the door
As I open it, a familiar face I see
The father I love is home once more.

Kathleen Morrison (10)
Airidhantuim Primary School, Shader, Isle of Lewis

The Jungle

In the jungle, where it's hot and stuffy
A panda stands so cute and fluffy

While eating long green leaves
His monkey pals are swinging on trees

The snakes slither through the grass
And the lions roar as they pass

As the tigers stroll by
Colourful parrots fly in the sky

Insects scuttle along dead tree stumps
While koalas climb up tall tree trunks

Crocodiles snap with their long narrow jaws
And rainbow lizards sharpen their claws

While the hyenas are at play
Everyone goes to sleep for the day.

Gemma MacDonald (11)
Airidhantuim Primary School, Shader, Isle of Lewis

The Snow

The snow is an awesome, piercing sight
With its magnificently bright white
From the clouds it floats down
Adding sparkle to the grey and brown

The brilliant white on the mountain peak
Looks very cold, bitter and bleak
Against the skyline it catches your eye
Glinting in the sunshine as the birds fly by

Each snowflake has its own matchless design
So small and delicate, fragile and fine
How many snowflakes blanket the ground?
Before they melt and can no longer be found?

Zoe Smith (10)
Airidhantuim Primary School, Shader, Isle of Lewis

Night

At night
I hear
Bats squeaking
Cats purring
I stop!

I see a light outside
So I take my torch
There is something moving
In the porch

I put the light against it
I can't believe my eyes
My cat and dog are fighting
Are they dead or alive?

I tell them to be quiet
So they don't cause a riot
That's what it is like
At night!

Catriona Rennie (7)
Airidhantuim Primary School, Shader, Isle of Lewis

Henrik Larsson

See Larsson sprinting down the field
Dribbling the ball past the defenders
Dodging and darting through the players
Scoring a goal for Barcelona

The crowd roaring as the ball hits the net
Raising his arms when he celebrates
Another win for his team
Man of the match once again.

Murray MacDonald (8)
Airidhantuim Primary School, Shader, Isle of Lewis

Night

When my mum leaves the room
And switches off the light
I call down, 'Ceitlin
Come on quickly
Let's have a pillow fight'

Mum yells, 'What are you doing?'
And gives us a fright!
I leap under the covers
Ceitlin sprints up the stairs

I count the hairs in my head
Until I fall asleep in bed
I drift into a dream
For eternity it seems.

Micheil Russell Smith (9)
Airidhantuim Primary School, Shader, Isle of Lewis

My Family

There are six in our house counting me
Mum, dad, two sisters and my brother
When we're together we make a lot of noise
And keep bumping into each other

Dad works late every night
While Mum cooks the tea
Chloe plays her music very loud
And Livvy paints a tree

My brother Dael reads lots of books
To do with ships and planes
So you see there are a lot of us
Johnson is our name.

Charlotte Johnson (7)
Airidhantuim Primary School, Shader, Isle of Lewis

The Wacky Witch's Curse

As I heard screams from a hole
I hoped it might be a blind mole
But no it was much worse
It was Wacky Witch conducting a curse

From the hole, smoke came out
And spread a smell round about
But nosily I stayed to hear
Despite my shaking in alarming fear

As I heard evil chuckles
I began to gnaw my knuckles
Hoping she wouldn't appear
But I felt her presence near

And her curse I heard her chant
Mutters foul in her rave and rant
I knew it was time to go
But which way, I didn't know

I crept away scared to the bone
In any direction to a safe zone
For I knew there was nothing worse
Than to be under the Wacky Witch's curse!

Heather Donnelly (11)
Airidhantuim Primary School, Shader, Isle of Lewis

Night

I go to bed, wanting to sleep
But all I hear are the boys, out on the street
Playing, shouting, by the silver moon
I hope I'll be able to go to sleep soon

The stars are out, shining bright
I get up to the window to close the curtains tight
The night freaks me out, the shadows loom
I hope I'll be able to go to sleep soon

I go under the covers and put them over my head
Thinking of ghosts going round my bed
I'm really scared, even though it's not cool
I hope I'll be able to get to sleep soon

I want to dream of lots of money
And of clowns which are very funny
To ride in a carriage of gold it would seem
It's alright now, I've started to dream.

Sandra Corbett (11)
Airidhantuim Primary School, Shader, Isle of Lewis

My Cat

My cat isn't flat
My cat isn't fat
My cat isn't yellow
My cat doesn't bellow

My cat isn't bright
My cat isn't light
My cat isn't chummy
My cat isn't funny

My cat is puffy
My cat is fluffy
My cat is a male
My cat is only a tale!

Harpa McTaggart (12)
Airidhantuim Primary School, Shader, Isle of Lewis

Simpsons

The Simpsons is a funny show
And everyone who's seen it should know
In The Simpsons, Homer says 'Doh!'
And his favourite bartender is Moe
At the nuclear power plant, Homer has a job
Bart's enemy is known as Sideshow Bob
Bart always gets into trouble
But for entertainment it is more than double
Bart's idol is Krusty the Clown
And he never lets Bart frown
There is an Indian called Apu
And he is a Hindu
A Scotsman called Willie
Acts very silly
Marge has blue hair
And treats Maggie with tender care
Lisa plays the saxophone
And produces a lovely tone
Most Simpsons are coloured yellow
The creator Matt Groening is a funny fellow.

Connor Mackay (10)
Airidhantuim Primary School, Shader, Isle of Lewis

Bats

Flying in the night
Giving people a fright
Hiding in the trees
Hovering like bees
An oily black coat
His wings are like a cloak

Looks like a rat with wings
Doesn't really have a lot of things
Big long teeth
Sucking into beef.

Alex Maitland (9)
Ballasalla Primary School, Isle of Man

Sweet Shop

Lollipop, lollipop sweet and sour
Like a fizzy sherbet on a stick
Everything's gone in an hour
Except the things you lick

Chewing my bubblegum
I love all chocolates especially dairy milk
Bubblegum is the best, yum, yum
I like Galaxy because it reminds me of silk

There are lots of shelves of all kinds of sweets
There are sweets called love hearts
There are some sweets that are shaped as seats
There are some sweets called jelly tarts.

Rohana Quereshi (10)
Ballasalla Primary School, Isle of Man

Footballers

Footballers, footballers how do you kick?
Footballers, footballers how do you shoot?
Footballers, footballers how do you do it?
Footballers, footballers what is your team?
Footballers, footballers.

Jason Collister (10)
Ballasalla Primary School, Isle of Man

Mums

Mums, why are you so mean?
I'm gonna leave you when I am eighteen
If I don't you will scream, when you are playing my scene
When I am nineteen, in golf I will get par
Then I will jump a car and then get a scar.

Rhys Quayle (9)
Ballasalla Primary School, Isle of Man

Spider, Spider

Spider, spider
Sitting on the wall
Spider, spider
Webbing the hall
Spider, spider
Having a bath

Spider, spider
Having a snooze
Spider, spider
Webbing my bed
Spider, spider
Electric head

Spider, spider
Found the shed
Spider, spider
Messing my head
Spider, spider
Going to shoot you dead.

Jake Grimshaw (9)
Ballasalla Primary School, Isle of Man

My Greedy Little Sister

Aero bars
Chocolate stars
Jelly tots
Sweet in knots
Easter eggs
Frogs on legs
Bubblegum
Toffee rum
All in Kayleigh's tummy
'Mummy my tummy hurts!'

Imogen Cannell (10)
Ballasalla Primary School, Isle of Man

Spiders

Crawling up the wall
Sticking on the roof
Biting its lunch with its sharp tooth
Scaring little kids
Crawling up armpits

Eight black, hairy legs
Little scary eyes
Black hairy, chest
Clear, see-through blood.

Jack Garrett (9)
Ballasalla Primary School, Isle of Man

Hamster

Hamsters can run in their tube
Hamsters can run in their wheel
Hamsters can nibble food very fast
Hamsters can play funny games
Hamsters can chew things
Hamsters can roll about
Hamsters have short woolly coats

Are hamsters playful and quiet?

Abigail Jones (9)
Ballasalla Primary School, Isle of Man

The Cut Sheep

The cut sheep fell into a heap
And broke its teeth
I said, 'How can you eat?'
It said, 'I don't know
But the heap was very deep and I would like
Some meat to eat.'

Andrew Corkill (10)
Ballasalla Primary School, Isle of Man

The Game Of Football

I can hear the roar of the crowd
As I whack the ball up the pitch
Shouting and screaming, 'Shoot!'
As my team mate gets hacked

The thumping of my heart
We got a penalty as I get chosen to take it
This is a chance of a lifetime to be a hero
Nerves are starting . . . everyone is depending on me

I put the ball on the spot, everyone was quiet
The whistle blew, I start running up to the ball
I hit the ball, I followed up and watched the ball
The keeper went the other way, I scored

Everyone came over to me to congratulate me
The crowd was cheering and shouting
My manager said, 'You're definitely in the team'
We went to the changing rooms, we'd won 1-0.

Laura Beggs (10)
Ballasalla Primary School, Isle of Man

Since You Went Away

Since you went away
Your balls have just been lying on the ground
And your lead and collar have just been sitting in a plastic bag
Your basket is lying on the floor with no dog in it
Since you went away
Things have been sad instead of jolly
And there is no jumping dog around

But now we have a new dog called Sasha
She's just like you Sharday
But a little smaller and a different colour coat
But still sometimes I stop and think of you
And also the house is jolly once again and everyone is happy.

Lauren Gelling (10)
Ballasalla Primary School, Isle of Man

The Will And The Word

You whisper the words
The sorcery boils inside
Then . . . it is unleashed

It seeks out victims
When found, finally it explodes
It destroys their soul

Blood squirts everywhere
Inner organs whirl around
Grey eyes stare blankly

It's a predator
Seeking for unwary prey
As quick as lightning

Death stands before it
Immeasurable power
Is yours forever

Though, using magic
Obliterates energy
Until after rest.

Terence Lennon (9)
Ballasalla Primary School, Isle of Man

Football

As I ran down the line
With the ball at my feet
I passed it to my mate called Pete
He was going to shoot but he lost his boot
So he went back for it as I got the ball
But it went too high and it hit the wall
But luckily the other player had a fall
And I was very happy when the match was done because
I could have a hot cross bun.

Billy Harris (10)
Ballasalla Primary School, Isle of Man

My Kitten Likes To Sleep In Mum's Handbag!

My kitten likes to sleep in Mum's handbag
So one day my mum got a fright
As my mum was going to a party
Till the middle of the night

My kitten likes to sleep in Mum's handbag
Slithering like a snake
Into his nest he goes
No noise he makes

He is as orange as fire
And white as snow
He is as bouncy as a ball
But you wouldn't know

My kitten likes to sleep in Mum's handbag.

Breeshey Mort (9)
Ballasalla Primary School, Isle of Man

My Brother

Annoying selfish brat
Who is taking a while to adapt
He eats with his mouth open at tea
And always makes fun of me

Annoying selfish brat
He never shuts his mouth at that
He swears he doesn't lose things
But I know he thinks they've got wings

But no matter how much he annoys me
And is like a talking bee
I'll always love him dearly
And hopefully, he'll love me.

Mason McLarney (9)
Ballasalla Primary School, Isle of Man

Joly!

Joly was an old dog
She lived for 17 years
But on her 17th birthday
There were puddles of soggy tears

We went on a trip to England
To bury her in her grave
We put flowers all around it
And spread tears on the pavement

We all sat down and thought
About her cheerful days
The way that she caught the ball
And slobbered on her ways

She looked so very cute
With her fluffy pricked up ears
She looked a bit like a fox
Only she had no fears

My dog Joly!

Kelly Firth (9)
Ballasalla Primary School, Isle of Man

Cats

Cats play with lots of wool
Cats are vivacious
Cats can run like foxes

Cats like to catch mice
Cats like to jump high
Cats like to be with you
Aren't cats cute?

Dinah Cain (9)
Ballasalla Primary School, Isle of Man

Things Have Changed

Things have changed now
You're not around
Things are not lively anymore
Outside is dull
Since you went away

Your bowls are still here, lying on the ground
All damp and wet, never to be seen again
Around things have changed
Your purring in the garden
Is never to be heard again

Your rug you used to lie on, is no use to us now
My dear cat Raven, is never to be seen again.

Anna Watterson (9)
Ballasalla Primary School, Isle of Man

Empire State Building

Standing tall
Once above all

Looking across at Liberty
Looking down at mingling crowds

High above all his brothers
Raising their faces in praise

Inside: the glare of man-made brightness
Outside: the glow of natural sun

Once taller than all
Now stunted by others
Once filled with pride
Now riddled with melancholy.

David Milligan (11)
Cargilfield School, Edinburgh

Twinkling Surprise

A surprise is a twinkling star
Hiding in the dark
Ready to shine its golden light
With a smile on your face

A surprise paints a smile
An enormous cheek to cheek smile
With eyes glittering in delight
But do not let it out of your sight and
Protect and care for it like a baby

The little star starts losing its light
For no attention or care comes its way
A week or two and the light has vanished
Behind the dark veil of familiarity

Yet, waiting silently for another chance to shine its light
And bring another golden smile
An enormous cheek to cheek smile . . .
Is the next surprise

But how long will it then last?
Until its light has faded into the darkness of acquaintance
Again . . . and again!

Ailie Corbett (11)
Cargilfield School, Edinburgh

Dogs

I see the huge dog
Snarling and barking at me
I am quite afraid

I love the wee pup
Tugging and pulling my hand
I am having fun!

Tom Younger (12)
Cargilfield School, Edinburgh

Brush Your Teeth!

B ites of chocolate and crunchies
R usting your teeth
U se your toothbrush
S crub them hard even if it's
H urting you

Y orkshire pudding is
O h so delicious - just like
U pside down eggs. But
R otting

T eeth and
E normous holes of decay can
E ventually follow. But I must have
T he triple-tiered cake
H ot from the bakery!

Lalsa Budhwar (10)
Cargilfield School, Edinburgh

The Seasons

Sun shines in summer
But brown leaves fall in autumn
The year seeps away

Snow falls in winter
Now children play in springtime
The year lives again!

Joanna Scott (10)
Cargilfield School, Edinburgh

Retreat!

Our attack is halted
Somebody shouts *retreat*
We sprint like hell-bent rats towards our trench
The deathly rattle of the monstrous machine gun starts up
Piercing our hearts

Dead bodies lie limp in the dry mud
Then bombing starts: *boom!*
Earth shaking
Men - screaming, shouting, falling, dying . . .

But still I run on
Our captain shouts, 'Hit the dirt!'
All dive for cover except me
I call out like a drowning man
Nobody hears . . .

Pain overwhelms me
I call out once again
But the only reply is a gurgle of blood
Followed by blackness and nothing . . .

I wake!
Am I dead or am I alive?
I am in a hospital bed
I scream in agony as I clutch my leg
I am comforted by a nurse
I gasp for breath
I'm sick again . . .

I hear a doctor whispering, 'Will he live through the night?'

Now it dawns on me
The reality of war.

Geordie Milne (10)
Cargilfield School, Edinburgh

Fire Alarm

In class; 5.15pm
I hear the blaring screech of the fire alarm!
There is a hustle and bustle on the stairs
It never seems to end
The front door opens
The freezing wind from outside blows in . . .

Outside the afternoon is dark as night
We - standing in lines, straight as arrows
The frosty air makes us numb all over
It feels like hypothermia!

I start to get bored and annoyed
What's taking so long
To fix the fire problem?

Max Rasmusen (10)
Cargilfield School, Edinburgh

Trees

Gnarled branches
Grope in the wind

Leaves of yellow, ochre, red and green
Dance to the sodden ground

The trunk stands high and proud
As eerie whispers blow down on me

But in the silence of a windless day
It stands solitary and lonely

It seems to stare disconsolately
Down at me

And I -
I open my arms in a warm welcoming embrace
As I touch the coarse bark.

Isabella McMicking (11)
Cargilfield School, Edinburgh

My Pet Dog

I have a dog called UJ
He is always hungry
We have to give him lots of food
But my dog loves to walk
My dad never forgets UJ's toy

UJ's toy is a ball on string
When we come back my dog is muddy
We have to put my muddy dog in the bath
When he is clean he leaves hairs in the bath
My mum cleans the bath with water

My dog is fluffy and soft
His colour is good as brown, black and white
I love my dog UJ he is a sheepdog
I love him with my heart.

Jade Parsons (9)
Darley Dale Primary School, Matlock

Vehicles

Vehicles can go very fast
Soft tops can go even faster
Lorries can't go very fast at all
Normal cars go half-way

Rally cars go over the limit
They go very fast and sometimes crash
They make a lot of noise like this: *vroom, vroom!*

Soft top cars can take their roofs off
They also have twin exhausts
They can go up to 200mph I think.

Jordan Crapper (8)
Darley Dale Primary School, Matlock

My Goldfish

My goldfish swim all day long
Waiting for me to come from school
My mum says she feeds them and cleans the tank out
But sometimes I don't really believe her
At 5.30pm I give them their food
They sometimes don't eat it because they're in a mood
My fish are the colour of gold
They have slits in their body that are gills
I think that they're asleep because they're still
We better not wake them from their nap
For they need their rest for a big day ahead
I have to clean the tank out every week
I have to make sure the filter doesn't leak
My fish like to watch TV
They like to watch it with me
My goldfish talk to each other
They try to talk to me
I'm very happy, I have them
Swimming next to me.

Hannah Richardson (9)
Darley Dale Primary School, Matlock

Rally Cars

Sometimes skidding, sometimes crashing
The people shouting in the crowd
Being wild and jumping around
Rally cars so fast 110 miles per hour
Whizzing around like mad
Bouncing about navigation rock-hard helmets
Taking your head side to side
Bumping together.

Kalen Rhodes (8)
Darley Dale Primary School, Matlock

My Poppy

I have a dog called Poppy
I care for her of course
I like it when she waggles her tail at me

My dog has a coat
A hat
A collar and a teddy called Tigger

Poppy has a cosy bed
A nice warm blanket and another ted

We brush her hair with a nice brown brush
She likes it I can tell

Poppy eats carrots, bones and drinks water

That's my Poppy.

Laura Mosley (8)
Darley Dale Primary School, Matlock

My Cat

My cat is a boy
And he has lots of toys
He likes to sleep, sleep, sleep
And he likes to peep, peep, peep through doors

His colour is black and white
And sometimes he can bite
If we leave him alone he's alright

If anytime he sees something move
He sits and just watches it
Until it gets round the corner then pounces onto it

I love my cat
And it's so cute.

Jade Boswell (8)
Darley Dale Primary School, Matlock

Rally Cars

Rally cars racing with their noisy engines
Vroom, vroom, vroom!
Puffing out smoke
And *screeching* round corners
Sometimes *crashing* into things

People come to watch them
On different types of surfaces
Bounding over jumps
And splashing the audience

Racing all over the world
They get knocked and squashed
And have lots of types of chassis
Using different types of hydraulics

All different types of colours and shapes
Bright headlights roam the lands
With big windscreens
Winning races and prize money.

James McDonald (9)
Darley Dale Primary School, Matlock

Rabbits

Rabbits are my friends
Because they make me giggle
I like rabbits because they are cute and
Cuddly and because they are furry and hairy
Rabbits are fun to play with
In their hut they need hay and straw.

Sarah Pritty (8)
Darley Dale Primary School, Matlock

My Imaginary Friend

Lisa's my best friend
Mum and Dad say she's only pretend
She plays with me everyday
We slide down the slide we jump in the hay
She eats dirty yellow grass
The teachers at school say, 'Oh what a clever lass'
When she jumps on my bed
I get told off, because Mum thinks Lisa's not real
She doesn't talk much
But there's one thing I'll never forget
When she said her father was Dutch
She walks really fast
Though at sports day at the races she always comes last
But I've got to admit, but keep it a secret
Lisa's my imaginary friend.

Jessica Greatorex (8)
Darley Dale Primary School, Matlock

Seasons

Seasons, seasons are very nice
Summer is the hottest season
Spring and autumn, they are quite hot
Winter is the coldest season
Summer is very sticky
Spring is when the lambs are born
Autumn is when the flowers open wide and
The leaves fall from the trees
Winter is very cold, it can snow in winter
The snow can be very thick or it can be thin.

Emily Cunningham (8)
Darley Dale Primary School, Matlock

My Fish

My fish is the best ever
Her name is Izzie
She's gold with black spots
Until she died in October 2004

After school I came running home to find her
But she's not there
I didn't know why she died
Was it the food or the water?
I knew it was the water
I haven't cleaned it out for days

My sister had a fish as well
His name was Bubbles
Oh why did they have to die?

Sophie Birds (8)
Darley Dale Primary School, Matlock

My Hamster

My hamster bites a lot, I don't like him
He's like a sheepdog, black and white
He climbs his cage trying to get out but he can't

His name is Harry
He lives in a cage
And he always stays in bed but when I come he jumps out
Of his bed and he lets me stroke him

I'm lucky I've got Harry, he's so playful and he
Deserves a stroke every time
He's so tiny, he can fit through my finger and my thumb making a hole.

Jonathan Goodwin (8)
Darley Dale Primary School, Matlock

Seasons

Seasons are great
Seasons are the best
These are all the seasons
Summer
Winter
Autumn
Spring
Summer is hot
Winter is cold
Autumn is a mixture
Spring is the same
In autumn all the leaves fall off the trees
When it is spring, the leaves are back
Into a nice, greeny colour.

Katie Wheeldon (8)
Darley Dale Primary School, Matlock

A Friend

A friend is a person who looks after you
A friend is a person who you can turn to and
Always helps you if you need any help
A friend is a person who you can rely on to be there
If you need anybody to rely on
A friend is a person who comes round to your house
A friend cares for you and worries about you
You can go to them if you need help or advice
A friend is always there for you
You can be a good friend by caring for them and helping them
Are you a good friend?

Lucy Vaughan (8)
Darley Dale Primary School, Matlock

Vehicles

Vehicles drive down the street
And down to the main road
Where all the cars meet
There's a car that's being towed

Cars stop at a garage and fill up with petrol or it
Might be diesel
I saw a lorry run over a weasel

A lorry reverses onto the road
The driver looks out for cars
Carrying a heavy load
He looks out the window and up to Mars.

Joe Marsden (9)
Darley Dale Primary School, Matlock

Manchester United

Manchester United have Nistelrooy, Rooney and Giggs
They turn out in red, black and white
Their mascot is called the red devil
Their rival is Man City who are in the premiership like Man U
Their stadium is called Old Trafford
They won the FA Cup
They have up to 69,000 seats
Their manager is called Sir Alex Ferguson, can be quite strict
They also have some more players like
Alan Smith, Luis Saha, Christiano Ronaldo and
Tim Howard the goalkeeper.

Charlie Short (8)
Darley Dale Primary School, Matlock

My Best Budgie

It flies smoothly
At the speed of 20 miles per hour
It lands softly
Spreads it's wings out like somebody stretching
As they've been napping forever and a day
It starts flying again
As I run into the room
He follows me
I cannot live without my budgie.

Connor Roulston (9)
Darley Dale Primary School, Matlock

The Leopard

The leopard prowls around its prey,
It is dark but nearly day.
He takes two steps, stops, sniffs and smells,
Picks up the scent of some gazelles.

He spots their horns in the reedy grass,
Crouches down and lets them pass.
He stalks them stealthily, taking care
That his victims stay unaware.

The leopard now increases his pace,
Concentration on his face.
He chooses a youngster, on the right,
Prepares to spring with all his might.

The leopard pounces at its prey,
The gazelle hears him and swerves away.
The hunt has failed yet again
And all his efforts have been in vain.

Toyah Metcalfe (8)
Dawpool CE (Aided) Primary School, Wirral

Midnight Moon

Creeping
Crawling across the night sky
The sun is her husband
Stars are her children
I like to watch the way you fly
Shining light over the land

Searching
Looking for the North star
The wind gets cold
Darker are the clouds
She knows she can't be far
But the night starts to grow old

Setting
Down she glides
The sun comes up
Rises quickly with big strides
The moon has disappeared for another day.

Philippa Conlon (10)
Dawpool CE (Aided) Primary School, Wirral

The Blind Horse

There once was
A horse who was
Big and kind but
The sad thing was he was blind
He bumped into walls
He tripped over balls
What a poor horse he was
He tried and he tried
But sadly he died.

Jessica Greenwood (8)
Dawpool CE (Aided) Primary School, Wirral

Seven Little Children

Seven little children making a house of sticks
One fell over, then there were six!

Six little children playing with a beehive
One got stung, and then there were five

Five little children slamming a door
One got his finger trapped, then there were four

Four little children having a cup of tea
One was sick, then there were three

Three little children lining up for the loo
One took too long, then there were two

Two little children ran away from number one
He got lonely then there were none.

Harriet Dool (9)
Dawpool CE (Aided) Primary School, Wirral

My Dog Tess

My dog Tess is gorgeous and fluffy
She runs round the garden and gets very muddy

She runs all day she plays all night
She's as fast as an airplane, so she gives me a fright

She lies in her kennel, she eats all her food
She's very easy going she won't get in a mood

Tess is my warm cosy blanket, who keeps me warm at night
She sneaks in my bedroom, she plays with my hair
And when she's had enough she cuddles up with my bear!

I love her always forever I'll care
When I need a friend she'll always be there.

Kate Howard (8)
Dawpool CE (Aided) Primary School, Wirral

Nanna

I love her and she loves me
Because we're one big happy family
I advised her then, I miss her now
And that won't change a bit
Not when I'm around anyhow
But there came a time she had to go
My heart won't stop
It will grow and grow
And that's how I remember her
Throughout my life I'll see her there
At the bottom of my heart together forever
I love her and she loves me
Because we're one big happy family.

Chrissy Howden (10)
Dawpool CE (Aided) Primary School, Wirral

The Playground

As I sit and ponder
I wonder what it will be
Skipping, tag or blockie
The choice is up to me

For I'm a playground leader
To start a game - that's me
To make sure they run smoothly
And everyone is free!

The bell has just rung
The playground is at peace
All the children are inside
And the gulls are left to feast.

Anna Lecoustre (10)
Dawpool CE (Aided) Primary School, Wirral

Summer Holidays

Hot summer holidays flip-flops on my feet
I might go on holiday but don't know who I'll meet
Picnics at the seaside, collecting pretty shells
Suntan cream and BBQs, my favourite summer smells
Flowers in the meadow blowing in the breeze
Lots of yellow pollen making people sneeze
People in the garden lots of things to do
A garden full of colours, yellow, pink and blue
Picking juicy strawberries in the summer heat
Having them for pudding
What a summer treat
Lazy summer evenings out playing with my friends
Oh how I love the summer
And I wish it never ends.

Elizabeth Frost (8)
Dawpool CE (Aided) Primary School, Wirral

The Adorable Pair

My two dogs have the same name as a tree
My two dogs are always playing with me

Bracken loves chewing a bone
Bracken's happy sleeping at home

Holly's name is like a prickly tree
Holly was a present just for me

Running or skipping they're by my side
But they would never be seen on a slide!

After they've been fed
They curl up in their cosy warm bed.

Elisha Ladell (9)
Dawpool CE (Aided) Primary School, Wirral

My Cat

His belly sags to the floor
That's my cat Sam

His favourite person is my Mum
That's my cat Sam

He sometimes plays, he usually sleeps
That's my cat Sam

My cat Sam is greedy and lazy
But I love him and that's what counts.

Carrie Taylor (8)
Dawpool CE (Aided) Primary School, Wirral

My Mum

My mum has a heart of gold
She's pretty well known anywhere
There's always food on the table
Whenever there's trouble she's always there
A hug is always there
But to be fair
She's a mum but
A special mum
My mum.

Jessica Scullion (9)
Dawpool CE (Aided) Primary School, Wirral

Trains

T rains go up and down the track all day
R ails side by side, parallel to each other
A ll different loads
I n all weather
N icer than travelling on other transport
S tation is near, time to stop!

Peter Morris (11)
Dawpool CE (Aided) Primary School, Wirral

Wonderful Snow

One winter morning, so cold and bitter
Robins chirping in the trees
Snowflakes falling on the ground
Snow smothered everywhere
On the houses, trees and all over the floor
Snowman dotted here and there
With a carrot as a nose

The snow is coming gently down
Landing on the smoothing ground
Little children coming out to play
Wrapped up nice and warm
With a hat, scarf and a coat

Whooshing down real fast
Down the snowy hills
On sleigh's blue and green
Under the snowy trees

But I guess it has come to an end
So the following day
The sun comes out to play
And makes the snow disappear
Till next year!

Rachel Brooker (11)
Dawpool CE (Aided) Primary School, Wirral

Things I Like About You

1. You're pretty, I'm gorgeous
2. You're the coolest kid in the school and I'm not
3. You find secrets that I don't even know about
4. You are the leader of all the games and I'm stuck at the back.
5. You get to stay in at playtime and I'm stuck outside
6. You find friends easy peasy and I'm just grateful I've got you
7. *You're the bestest friend I've ever known.*

Bethan Gee (8)
Dawpool CE (Aided) Primary School, Wirral

My Christmas List

Dear Santa, here's my Christmas list
I hope I can have it all
I've only asked for the gifts my parents
Can't find at the stores

I'd like to have a time machine
So I can go back in time
I'd also like world peace
Oh and please no more crime

A ten foot teddy bear
Is a present I could use
I'll also need a puppy dog
For that one
I'll let you choose

Please bring a gentle horse
That will let me ride it day and night
And don't forget a stable
And, yes a carriage would be a delight

I'll need a widescreen TV
And won't you please provide
A famous pop singer
That won't run and hide

Of course you can afford it
Because you are Santa
Oh and my sister has a wish
That only you can grant her!

Amy Wilkinson (10)
Dawpool CE (Aided) Primary School, Wirral

On A Moonlit Evening

On a moonlit evening
I was walking in the woods
When the moon went behind the clouds
And everything went dark and silent
Silent except for the pounding of hooves
Left, right, left, right
Coming closer and closer
Pounding through the trees
And crashing into my heart
The sound was getting closer and faster
Left, right, left, right
Beating an angry pattern
Until they were beside me
Leaping towards me
Then . . .
Then the moon came out, from behind the cloud
And a gentle breeze passed through me
And everything was calm again
And the hooves slowed down
Left, right, left, right
And as they beat their pattern
I felt . . . happy
Just happy that they were there
Like they were watching over me
Like . . . I was flying through the sky
But if I fell, someone would catch me
And as I ran from out the wood
I noticed on a cliff
A pure white stallion rearing up
Rearing at the moon . . . and me.

Laura Helsby (10)
Dawpool CE (Aided) Primary School, Wirral

Fairies

Jack Frost one day told the fairies, 'Go away!'
They were very cross
They said, 'He's not the boss'
'I am the boss and you will see you'll have to listen to me'
'Not on your nelly,' the fairies said
Then sent Jack Frost straight to bed
So we will leave Jack Frost in bed
'I will never mess with those fairies,' he said
'I've had a dreadful fright
I'll stay right here tucked up tight.'

Annabel Webster (9)
Dawpool CE (Aided) Primary School, Wirral

Birds

Birds are great
They really like flying up
Up into the sky
Then back down to catch that fly
Then jump onto the bird table
Collect some bread
Then up to the nest
Where their chicks are in bed
Hungry little things
Chirping and a cheeping
Now they all are eating.

Millie Powell (7)
Dawpool CE (Aided) Primary School, Wirral

Swimming

Is it the thrill of the swim
Or the shrill of the whistle
My heart is pounding
My arms and legs are bounding
Gracefully we glide
Hoping not to collide
And all the time saying, 'Win, win, win'
Trainers screaming, 'Pull, pull, pull'
It looks like they're in for the kill
It not just about medals
It's not just about winning
It's all about swimming and swimming and swimming.

Anna Johnson (10)
Dawpool CE (Aided) Primary School, Wirral

Some People Are Very Funny

Some people are very funny
Some just cry and want their mummy
Some just sit and suck their dummy
Some eat sprouts
They think they're yummy
Some people are very funny
Some get cross nearly all the time
Some get moss and mix it with slime
I hope they don't do that all the time.

Jenny Davies (8)
Dawpool CE (Aided) Primary School, Wirral

From My Window

Early one morning
When birds are fast asleep
With the waves gently lapping upon the sand
And rowing boats bobbing up and down
I see mounts of grass in the distance
With brick upon brick of house
With lights switched off
And the roads so quiet and not a single car passing by
We all lie sleeping
While the morning breaks into light
And then it gets so busy
We don't think about the new morning that has just passed.

Lucy Bramhall (10)
Dawpool CE (Aided) Primary School, Wirral

Sorry, No Homework

During the weekend there was a frost,
And my pen and pencil turned to ice.
And my maths' book got inside a tornado.
I did my homework but the cat ate it.
I didn't do anything, (honest) when I looked around,
My art book fell in the washing machine
I don't know how.

My sister put my RE book in the fire,
And my ruler broke in half.
That's all I've go to say,
That's why I am not at school today.

Louisa Taylor (9)
Dickleburgh Primary School, Diss

Fire

Shining-brightly
Winter-glow
Streaming-colours
Warming-snow
Red-yellow
Orange-sparks
Lighting-nights
Incredibly-bright
Finally-dark.

Emma-Louise Harris (11)
Dickleburgh Primary School, Diss

Leprechaun

In Ireland I roam
I am a leprechaun now
From paddy to me.
My family misses me
But I don't miss them too much.

Benjamin Spinks (11)
Dickleburgh Primary School, Diss

Puppies - Haiku

The silly puppies
Puppies keep falling around
But I still love them.

Jak Kerry (10)
Dickleburgh Primary School, Diss

Lion Kennings

Sharp-teeth
Long-fur
Loud-roarer
Good-hunter
Very fierce
Very mean
Bone-cruncher
Flesh-tearer
Meat-eater
Scream-maker.

Hayden Wilby (10)
Dickleburgh Primary School, Diss

Blue Whale

Water-dasher,
Big-mouthed,
Barnacle-catcher,
Blue-beauty,
Sea-sweeper,
Fish-carer,
Sea-speaker,
Water-wonder,
Sea-queen.

Matthew Poll (11)
Dickleburgh Primary School, Diss

Rose

Oh so beautiful,
With dark red petals and thorns,
But under the shell,
Of its so dangerous form,
Is a delicate flower.

Craig Clark (11)
Dickleburgh Primary School, Diss

Homework

(Based on 'Dear Mum')

Sorry Miss

My homework just magically disappeared.
You wouldn't believe the night I had!
I had to watch my program that night,
It was the last episode, I couldn't miss it!
The pages became ruffled, when I had a bath.
The phone rang, which made me jump,
And yes you have guessed it,
My book fell in the bath.
I put it in the tumble dryer for one hour to dry out.
Of all the nights it was my turn to cook the tea,
Have you tried cooking baked beans on toast,
It takes sooo long to prepare you know!
The cat decided to fight with the dog,
There were fur balls everywhere, I couldn't hear myself think.
The rabbits broke out of their run.
Have you ever tried to catch three rabbits in the dark?
The sink leaked all over the floor,
Which blew a fuse in the dryer.
The radiators were covered in my sister's clothes.
The only place left was to hang it out to dry.
I had such a late night.
The alarm never went off.
We all got up late. (That's not good.)
My book, my book,
Where's my book?
Oh no!
It had disappeared off the line.

Sorry Miss

PS It's just a complete mystery!

Nicole Huggins (10)
Dickleburgh Primary School, Diss

The Ning Nang Nong

(Based on 'On the Ning Nang Nong' by Spike Milligan)

On the Nang Nong Ning
Where the snakes go ping
And the cows' shoes are blue
There's a Nang Ning Nong
Where the trees grow long
And the toasters all make stews
On the Nang Nong Ning
All the snakes go dang
And there are now very few in the zoo.

Oliver Wales (8)
Dickleburgh Primary School, Diss

The Nang Nong Ning

(Based on 'On the Ning Nang Nong' by Spike Milligan)

On the Nang Nong Ning
Where the pigs go ping
And the lions all go moo
There's a Nang Ning Nong
Where the snails are strong
And the cheetahs are very, very blue
On the Nong Ning Nang
All the hares go bang
And you just cannot see them when they do.

Oscar Stratton (8)
Dickleburgh Primary School, Diss

Man From Kent

There was a young man from Kent
Who had a big yellow tent
He went to his gran
In a big red van
That is the young man from Kent.

Daisy Holden (10)
Dickleburgh Primary School, Diss

Chocolate

(By a chocoholic)

Rich chocolate brownies
Milk chocolate buttons
Cold chocolate ice cream
And chocolate-topped muffins

Steamy hot chocolate
With cream on the top
Mint choc-chip lollies
And white chocolate drops

Chocolate spread sandwiches
Thick chocolate shake
Chilled chocolate mousse
And sticky chocolate cake

Chunky chocolate cookies
Thick chocolate custard
I'm going to invent
My own chocolate mustard

Steamed chocolate pudding
Makes my tummy rumble
Chocolate flakes through a straw
When they happen to crumble

In case you haven't noticed
Or you simply haven't heard
Chocolate is my most favourite thing
In the whole wide chocolate world.

Bronwyn Stratton (10)
Dickleburgh Primary School, Diss

Autumn Morning - Haiku

An autumn morning
The wind is blowing the leaves
Leaves float all around.

Steffan Wilby (7)
Dickleburgh Primary School, Diss

Journey To Pokémon Land

The king set off again, this time in a canoe
On his journey he saw his friend Sue
Then he found himself in Pokémon Land,
Where everyone likes Pikachu.

He asked, 'Who is the ruler here?'
'Machoke,' replied the Pokémon
'Thanks,' he said and off he went
To the palace they call Bon Con.

He saw their king called Pikachu,
He went to a café and ate a Tentacool,
He went to a place run by a Pokémon,
He found it was a Tetacruel.

He sailed home very merry,
And waved at Sue in his canoe
He felt a ball on his waist,
And shouted, 'Go sea canoe.'

Robert Payne (9)
Dickleburgh Primary School, Diss

Christmas

C hristmas is great fun.
H aving lots of presents to open.
R oast dinner at twelve o'clock.
I nviting all my family.
S anta left all the presents under the tree.
T hinking what presents I've got.
M ums work very hard at making lunch.
A nd happy faces when we open all our presents.
S weet dreams after the day is over.

Charlotte Theobald (10)
Dickleburgh Primary School, Diss

Journey To Cake Land

The king sailed away in a giant bowl,
The bowl had traces of rice,
And he found himself in Cake land,
Where everything is fattening and nice.

Before too long he saw a giant knife,
And ate a piece of chocolate cake.
His tummy bulged and grew so fat,
He had to burst it with a rake.

He went to a theme park,
And rode on a bun with a giant cherry.
Then he got on the strawberry swirl,
And he soon felt ever so merry.

He flew home on a plane,
All the way back to Paris
Where he looked up at the Trifle Tower,
Only to see Rolf Harris.

Danielle Clark (8)
Dickleburgh Primary School, Diss

Snake

Snake long and thin,
Slowly moves through the grass,
Hissing as he goes.
Step back and let him pass.

Carefully he picks out his prey,
Injects his victim with his fangs.
Crush, swallow,
There goes his meal.
Putting an end to his hunger pangs.
Snake long and fat drags himself through the grass,
Finds somewhere to sleep
Off his dinner until he's thin again.

Charles Pask (10)
Dickleburgh Primary School, Diss

Cheetah Kennings

Friend-eater
Long-haired
Sharp-teeth
Spotted-hunter
Quick-thinker
Fast-runner
Bone-cruncher
Caring-mother
Fierce-partner
Mean-leader
Silent-stalker
Angry-queen.

Caitlin Wade (10)
Dickleburgh Primary School, Diss

The Nang Nong Ning

(Based on 'On the Ning Nang Nong' by Spike Milligan)

On the Nang Nong Ning
Where the birds go bing
And the dogs all go coo
There's a Nang Ning Nong
Where the teachers are wrong
And the cats are all called Sue
On the Nong Ning Nang
All the rats say, 'Bang'
And the trees always have something to do.

Kieran Pask (8)
Dickleburgh Primary School, Diss

The Ning Nang Nong

(Based on 'On the Ning Nang Nong' by Spike Milligan)

On the Nang Nong Ning,
Where the crabs go ping,
And the sharks say, 'Moo moo,
There's a Nang Ning Nong,
Where the ants are long,
And teachers go wrong at the scary zoo,
On the Nong Ning Nang,
All the rats go bang,
And we just can't chase them when they do.

Natalie Leeder (9)
Dickleburgh Primary School, Diss

The Nang Nong Ning

(Based on 'On the Ning Nang Nong' by Spike Milligan)

On the Nang Nong Ning
Where the deers go cling
And all the cheetahs go moo
There's a Nang Ning Nong
Where the sea is strong
And the teachers are going to canoe
On the Nong Ning Nang
Rhinos hide in a gang
And you just can't find them but they find you!

Abigail Jones (8)
Dickleburgh Primary School, Diss

The Nang Nong Ning

(Based on 'On the Ning Nang Nong' by Spike Milligan)

On the Nang Nong Ning
Where the foxes wear bling
And ants jump like kangaroos
There's a Nang Ning Nong
Where the pythons grow strong
And the lamp posts all look wrong
On the Nong Ning Nang
All the leopards go bang
And the shops sell berry stew.

Liam Johnston (8)
Dickleburgh Primary School, Diss

The Nang Nong Ning

(Based on 'On the Ning Nang Nong' by Spike Milligan)

On the Nang Nong Ning
Where the lions go ping
And all the horses go coo
There's a Nang Ning Nong
Where the people sing a song
And the sky is never ever blue
On the Nong Ning Nang
All the cows go bang
And you just can't catch them when they do!

Esther Holden (7)
Dickleburgh Primary School, Diss

The Nang Nong Ning

(Based on 'On the Ning Nang Nong' by Spike Milligan)

On the Nang Nong Ning
Where the wasps don't sting!
And the pigs all have the flu
There's a Nang Ning Nong
Where the weeds all are very strong
And all the cookers are clean and new
On the Nong Ning Nang
All the rats go bang
And you just can't get passed them when they do!

Chloe Hines (9)
Dickleburgh Primary School, Diss

The Nang Nong Ning

(Based on 'On the Ning Nang Nong' by Spike Milligan)

On the Nang Nong Ning
Where the snakes all sing
And pigs go moo
There's a Nang Ning Nong
Where the leaves go bong
And the willow trees use kung fu
On the Nong Ning Nang
All the elephants will bang
And you can't catch them when they do!

Alexander Goodman (9)
Dickleburgh Primary School, Diss

The Nang Nong Ning

(Based on 'On the Ning Nang Nong' by Spike Milligan)

On the Nang Nong Ning
Where the pigs go ding
And kangaroos say boo
There in Nang Ning Nong
Where the teachers are wrong
All the tortoises say, 'Boohoo kangaroo'
On the Nong Ning Nang
All the birds sang bang
And elephants all go bong, bang, pong, pong.

Megan Chenery (8)
Dickleburgh Primary School, Diss

The Nang Nong Ning

(Based on 'On the Ning Nang Nong' by Spike Milligan)

On the Nang Nong Ning
Where the pigs still sing
The fish count up to twenty-two
There's a Nang Ning Nong
Where grass grows wrong
And the trees are covered in glue
On the Nong Ning Nang
All the worms go bang
And you can't bear it when they do.

Samantha Brimble (8)
Dickleburgh Primary School, Diss

The Nang Nong Ning

(Based on 'On the Ning Nang Nong' by Spike Milligan)

On the Nang Nong Ning
Where the snakes go bling
And the canaries all say, 'Moo'
There's a Nang Ning Nong
Where the fleas go mong
And the footballers never go boo
On the Nang Ning Nong
All the bees go pang
And you just can't catch them when they show.

Jack Chenery (9)
Dickleburgh Primary School, Diss

The Nang Nong Ning

(Based on 'On the Ning Nang Nong' by Spike Milligan)

On the Nang Nong Ning
Where the snakes all swing
And the lions all say 'Blue'
There's a Nang Ning Nong
Where the caws say hong kong
And the grass goes boo and then it sticks like glue
On the Nong Ning Nang
All the birds go clang
And you just can't catch them if they are blue.

Amanda Campbell White (8)
Dickleburgh Primary School, Diss

The Nang Nong Ning

(Based on 'On the Ning Nang Nong' by Spike Milligan)

On the Nang Nong Ning
Where the sharks say, 'Spring'
And fish are never blue
There's a Nang Ning Nong
Where horses go bong
And the curtains all say, 'Too, too, shoo, shoo'
On the Nong Ning Nang
All the cats go bang
And people do not like them when they do.

Bryony-Ann Cornish (7)
Dickleburgh Primary School, Diss

I Feel . . .

I feel afraid,
When I'm on a high building,
And am not able to find my way down.

I feel angry
When I get shouted at,
I turn around and go to my room.

I feel sad,
When I think about death,
It makes me want to cry.

But I feel happy, the best feeling of all,
Going to birthday parties,
That make me jump with joy.

Craig Rogers (11)
Donbank Primary School, Aberdeen

I Feel . . .

I feel afraid,
When I am flying on a plane,
High up in the sky in the clouds.

I feel angry,
When my dad turns off the TV,
And forgets to ask me first.

I feel sad,
When my sister breaks my things,
Because they are precious to me.

I feel happy, the best feeling of all,
When it is my birthday,
And friends give me presents.

Christopher Low (12)
Donbank Primary School, Aberdeen

I Feel . . .

I feel afraid,
When I'm on the back of a motorbike,
Going fast on the road with dad.

I feel angry,
When I get into trouble
At school, for doing nothing.

I feel sad
When someone hurts me,
And makes me feel very sore.

But I feel happy the best feeling of all,
When I go on holiday,
And play on the beach with my ball.

Tony Balbirnie (11)
Donbank Primary School, Aberdeen

I Feel . . .

I feel afraid,
When there is thunder and lightning,
And the noise makes me hide behind a chair.

I feel angry,
When people break my things,
Things that are special to me.

I feel sad,
When I am lonely,
And no one wants to play with me.

But I feel happy, the best feeling of all,
When my friends want to play with me,
Outside on the grass.

Lee-Anne Eddie (12)
Donbank Primary School, Aberdeen

Earth

E is for excited planet.
A is for asteroids blasting past.
R is for roaring seas.
T is for turbulent clouds.
H is for howling winds flying past.

Ryan Andrew (9)
Greenwards Primary School, Moray

Planet Mars

M is for Mount Olympus
A is for angry red rocks
R is for radar looking for water
S is for spacecraft landing on Mars.

Callum Edwards (8)
Greenwards Primary School, Moray

Green

Green is for really, really ill at hospital
Green is for the iris of your eyes
Green is for pepper just grown ripe,
Green is for broccoli I just don't like
Green is for bitter tasting pepper,
Green is for the puny praying mantis,
Green is for smelly scented seaweed,
Green is for soft gentle lullabies.

Matthew Knox (9)
Greenwards Primary School, Moray

Sunshine

S izzling eggs on the frying pan ground
U nder the palm tree with a lot of shade
N uggets of sunshine on your cheeks
S teaming eggs are now laid
H appy girls running on the hot sand
I nferno of heat shining on the land
N ight-time is so hot I have a little nap
E njoy the warmth of sunshine, as it gets ready for another lap.

Sam Mackenzie (8)
Greenwards Primary School, Moray

A Storm In Hawaii

A black cape of cloud covers the sky,
A sunny evening turns into a black midnight of storms,
Lightning crashing across the sky,
A stampede of 300 lions could not match the sound,
Little balls of water hit the window as I watch the storm go by.

Emily Tawse (9)
Greenwards Primary School, Moray

A Storm Over The Sea

The storm rushed towards the sea like a hurricane,
Rocking the sea to and fro
Hiding the sun,
Lightning crackled like shaking a can of Iron Bru and opening it,
The thunder roared like boulders falling off a mountain,
Cold, arctic drops of snow covered the grass.

Ciaran McLachlan (8)
Greenwards Primary School, Moray

Red

Red is for embarrassed when you go to choir
Red is for your heart pumping up and down around my body
You can smell sweet red strawberries
Red sweet berries swimming over to my nose.
Red is for strawberry juice, watering in my mouth
Red foxes creeping in my garden
Red, sweet roses juicy and beautiful
Red is for romantic music, when it's Valentine's Day.

Ashleigh Moir (8)
Greenwards Primary School, Moray

Planet Poem

N is for next to Pluto.
E is for Eighth planet in space
P is for peaceful and a quiet planet
T is for turning round in space.
U is for universe, enormous to look at.
N is for night blue sky
E is for energy spinning round and round.

Tracy Stuart (8)
Greenwards Primary School, Moray

Sunshine

S unshine is lovely but very hot
U nderneath the umbrella it's not
N apping in the shade I lie relaxing
S corching in the open sun goes in my eye.
H eat from the sun batters my face
I t feels intense upon my face.
N uggets of sun, nip my cheeks
E vening lands upon the sun.

Lauren Smith (8)
Greenwards Primary School, Moray

Icicles

I cy chilly wind blows against my face.
C limbing icicles form into lots of different shapes.
I nteresting icicles melt while the sunglows.
C ringing snow freezes my skin.
L ovely sun shining on the icicles, making colourful light.
E xcellent sun shimmering, making me not cold but hot.
S haped icicles glisten in the midday sun.

Alisha Sim (8)
Greenwards Primary School, Moray

A Storm In A Scottish Field

A storm sneaked into the sky, dragging its jet-black winter cloak
Lightning crackled loudly,
Lightning danced across the sky,
Thunder echoed like a lion's roar in a cave.
Rain hissed like a cat,
Icy, plump drops drenched the grass.

Rebecca Morrison (8)
Greenwards Primary School, Moray

Dragon Birth

In the dawn dew
A long time ago
On a far-off misty clearing
There was an enormous pit . . .

In the pit there were leaves,
Past those leaves there was mud,
Under that mud there was a nest,
On that nest there was a big dragon
Under that dragon there was an egg
On that egg there was a crack
From that crack

Came *dragon.*

Aimee Thorburn (8)
Greenwards Primary School, Moray

Red Poem

Red is for when your enraged at someone
Red is for your heart pumping blood into your veins.
Red is for the smell of wine.
Red is for a tasty red apple.
Red is for the sweet taste of raspberries.
Red is for a disgruntled bull.
Red is for a tulip in the flowerbed.
Red is for the sound of rock.

Cameron Milne (8)
Greenwards Primary School, Moray

My Dragon

I have a fighting dragon
He has a long tail like a sausage
If you call him any names, you will find a lot of pain
But he always plays with me every day.

Andrew Donoghue (8)
Greenwards Primary School, Moray

Dragon Birth

In the morning fog
Of long ago
In a far off misty clearing
There stood
A scary wood . . .

In the misty clearing
There grew a scary wood
Beneath the wood
There slunk a cave
And in that cave
The mosses grew
Beneath the mosses
There sat a rock
Beneath the rock
There sat an egg
And in that egg
There was a crack
And from that crack . . .

Dragon came.

Emily Coull (8)
Greenwards Primary School, Moray

My Dragon

I have a dopey dragon
With a big gold tail that bangs
And if anyone calls me names,
Goon touches his heart after his fangs.

So if you say I'm rubbish at football
Or call my hair messy
You might just get eaten up
And end up in his big belly.

David Smith Walker (8)
Greenwards Primary School, Moray

Dragon Birth

In the morning dew,
Of long ago
On a far-off mountainside,
There stood,
A wild wet forest . . .

In the wild, wet forest
There grew an oak tree,
Under the oak,
There was a cave,
And in that cave,
The grass grew long,
Beneath the grass,
There lay a heavy rock
Beneath that rock, there lay a dragon egg,
And in that egg,
There was a little crack,
Out of that crack, fire came,
From that fire,

Dragon came.

Lauren Fraser (9)
Greenwards Primary School, Moray

Red Poem

Red is angry, furious and frustrated,
Red is my blood running from the heart,
Red is for the smell of the red rose swaying in the breeze,
Red is strawberries that are my favourite fruit,
Red is the strawberry juice tasting so sweet,
Red is for a red squirrel running around,
Red is for the lovely tulip lying in the garden,
Red is for love music on Valentine's Day.

Rebecca Thom (8)
Greenwards Primary School, Moray

My Dragon

I have an evil green dragon,
His name is Scruff,
He has a long steel tongue
And a golden tail
He has frosty fangs and silver claws.

So if you tell me I am a peanut brain,
He will bite your head off!
Or say I am rubbish at maths
You just might see his bad side,
He has got fire you know!

If you come out to play with me,
You might get to play with my dragon.

Cieran Geddes (9)
Greenwards Primary School, Moray

Red Poem

Red is the blissful colour of silver
Red is for the heart that pumps blood around the body
Red is the sweet taste of berries
Red is for the red fox in the wood
Red is the sweet smelling rose
Red is for the red drum's beat in my ear.

Angus Lawson (8)
Greenwards Primary School, Moray

A Storm In A Hawaii Island

The surprise storm drifted across the misty atmosphere.
The lightning was emerging like plates crashing together.
The rumbling thunder cracks in the inky sky.
Scattering rain smacks hardly on the ground.

Ross Morrison (9)
Greenwards Primary School, Moray

A Storm In The Sea

A black cloak was forced across the sky
Bringing a dark, dull storm
Lightning danced across the sky like evil ballerinas
The thunder roared in my ears and gave me a headache.

The rain soaked me from head to toe
I stood there freezing watching the ship, away in the distance.

Lauren McLeary (9)
Greenwards Primary School, Moray

Red

Red is fury as people whisper
Red is the heart keeping us alive
Red is the rose that is hiding
Red is the watermelon so juicy
Red is the fox out in the night
Red is the chrysanthemum red as the heart
Red is the red rock music.

India Arbuthnott (9)
Greenwards Primary School, Moray

Playtime

People on the playground feeling happy,
Time to play, start jumping.

Playing football, doing gym
People racing, children win.

Basketballs bouncing, children swinging,
Cats running, dogs chasing.

Children skipping, leaves blowing,
Weather sunny, we had fun, now we have to go in.

Calum Pincombe (10)
Holway Park Primary School, Taunton

Sounds In The Park

In the park, children screaming,
Children playing happily, children crying.
The little kids kicking the balls in the air,
Big and little children on the swings, squeak, squeak.
Big kids flinging rubbish everywhere.
And you can hear children whooshing down the slides
As fast as they can.

Joshua Pennison (10)
Holway Park Primary School, Taunton

The Playground

The sun is shining and the children are screaming
The insects are crawling and the teachers are calling.
Throwing a rugby ball and kicking a football.
The flowers petals have been blown away
And the balls have been kicked a long, long, long way.
People playing tennis hitting balls over the fence.
Teachers worn out wishing they were at home.

Brooke Walsh (10)
Holway Park Primary School, Taunton

Playground

Playgrounds are for running, playing and hiding in the bushes
Jumping, cheering when score goals.
Shouting, screaming when the lob the ball
To the other side of the playground.
In the summer rolling jumping shouting and screaming
As the fields are getting hot the ice cream cools them down,
Through the summer days.
In the summer day at the end of the day,
When you see all children running away.

Chad Nixon (10)
Holway Park Primary School, Taunton

The Playground

The sun is shining,
The wind is blowing.

The spiders are crawling,
The worms are weaving.

The flowers are growing,
The trees are blowing.

The teachers are chatting,
The children are playing.

The footballs are flying,
The tennis balls are gliding.

The sun has gone in,
The moon has come out,
No more time to scream and shout.

Jessica Ward (10)
Holway Park Primary School, Taunton

Playtime

Boys in the playground, flinging rubbish,
And girls are tripping over.

Growing bluebells in the park
Trees are growing tall.

Children playing in the roundabout
Crying, giggling and smiling as they go around.

Insects crawling on the playground,
Children screaming and running away.

Boys are jumping up and down
Girls are skipping all around.

Connie Carter (9)
Holway Park Primary School, Taunton

Playground

Teachers shouting, 'Playtime, playtime'
Children running into the playground,
Some with footballs, some with skipping ropes
Playtime has started!

Footballs flying through the sky.
Some children laughing others crying,
As the rest are on the apparatus flipping and climbing.

The weather is sunny it's very hot,
Some children are sitting in the shade,
While some are spraying water everywhere.

Dinner ladies are shouting, 'Stop, stop'
As the two boys are scrapping on the floor.
The leaves are falling off the trees,
Trees are blowing in the blustering wind,
Birds are singing beautiful tunes,
While bees are buzzing all around.

Some children are making new friends, while others are falling out
Everyone is happy now playing all their games
But it's nearly 'in time'; there goes the bell, *ding dong!*

Kelly Pitt (10)
Holway Park Primary School, Taunton

At Playtime

The lesson's over playtime begins.
Run into the playground, where the fun begins.

Footballs are flying, teachers shouting.
Girls skipping and on the bar, children flipping.

The sun is shining, the leaves are falling.
Trees are swaying, and flowers blooming.

The bell is ringing and the children are moaning,
As they drop the footballs and skipping ropes
And walk sadly into class.

Zoe Portlock (10)
Holway Park Primary School, Taunton

Adults Say . . .

'Eat your dinner,'
'Don't talk,'
'Don't pick your nose,'
'Go to your room,'
'Go outside,'
'Go and play,'
'Have a bath,'
'Go to bed,'
'Don't touch the television,'
'Go away,'
'Don't touch your dog,'
'Go to the shops,'
'It's been a busy day,'
And my ears need a rest!

Callum Hooper (8)
Keynsham Primary School, Bristol

Adults

Adults say things like,
'Come here,'
'Don't talk,'
'Don't slop,'
'Go to sleep,'
'Have a bath,'
'Make a breakfast,'
'Sit down,'
'Shut up,'
'Go to your room,'
And that's not all
But I don't listen.

Ryan Sherborne (8)
Keynsham Primary School, Bristol

Evening Comes

Evening comes with
Moon shining brightly

Evening comes with
Stars twinkling softly

Evening comes with
Children washing noisily

Evening comes with
Owls hooting loudly

Evening comes with
People eating hungrily

Evening comes with
Babies sleeping happily

Evening comes with
Me watching quietly.

Chantelle Curtis (8)
Keynsham Primary School, Bristol

Friends

Friends say things like,
'Come out,'
'Come to the park,'
'Come down to the shop,'
'Come round the block with me,'
'Come in,'
'Come round,'
'Do you like me?'
'Have you got your bag?'
And I say, 'Yes.'

Nickeesham Griffiths (9)
Keynsham Primary School, Bristol

Pirates

Pirates say things like,
'You old rummy!'
'Where's my noggin of grog?'
'You old sea dog!'
'Walk the plank!'
'Where's my salt pork?'
'Scrub the deck!'
'Fire the canon!'
'Prepare the cabin.'
'Shiver me timbers!'
'You savvy!'
And I just say,
'Aye aye sir!'

James Bracey (9)
Keynsham Primary School, Bristol

The Old Pear Tree

The old pear tree is
A kite grabber
A pear grower
A granny shader
A bird carer
A wood maker
A bark holder
A nest holder
A leaf dropper
A paper maker
And most of all . . .
My favourite thing to climb.

Freya Bracey (7)
Keynsham Primary School, Bristol

Pirates Say

'Where's me rum?'
'Yar me hearties!'
'Walk the plank savvy!'
'Where's me food mate!'
'Scrub the deck!'
'Scrub the plank!'
'Shiver me timbers!'
But I just run away.

Daniel Harris (9)
Keynsham Primary School, Bristol

Teachers Say Things Like . . .

Teachers say things like
'Get on with your work,'
'Don't pick your nose,'
'Don't play with your ear,'
'Don't move your chair,'
'Stop eating your jumper,'
'Get outside now,'
And me not listening!

Chantelle Joyner (9)
Keynsham Primary School, Bristol

Night-Time

Night-time comes with Grandpa snoring
Night-time comes with owls flying
Night-time comes with people sleeping
Night-time comes with bats flying
Night-time comes with owls chasing mice
Night-time comes with mice squeaking
Night-time comes with rats running
Night-time comes with me tucked up in bed - reading.

Jack Burgoyne (8)
Keynsham Primary School, Bristol

Grandma's Cooking

Grandma is an awful cook, she bakes such awful cakes
Cherry cakes, cherryless and soft,
Fairy cakes, no icing and burnt,
Jam tarts with no jam or jelly,
Chocolate buns, burnt and hard,
Lemon cakes, curdled and crunchy
Coconut buns, cold and cracked
Chocolate cake, spicy and curried,
I ate them anyway.

Cory Mockridge (7)
Keynsham Primary School, Bristol

Mum

A tea maker
A bed straightener
A floor sweeper
A grass cutter
A hard worker
A TV watcher
And most of all a cuddle giver.

Daniel Shellard (7)
Keynsham Primary School, Bristol

Teachers

T eachers are nasty, green and mean
E veryone has an evil plan
A nd not a child has got away
C rying and scared, how the little children are
H airy, nasty and very bad smell
E very teacher is one
R ushing to get away from teachers
S o watch out you might be the next one.

Curtis Clack (10)
Lent Rise School, Burnham

Aliens In The Park

I once got told aliens lived in the park,
And had luminous glasses to see in the dark.
The person who told me was a little bit weird,
He was a really old man, with a great long beard.
When I got home I thought to myself,
What do aliens look like, do they have large ears like an elf.
That night I sneaked out to see with my eyes,
But out of a bush jumped a giant surprise,
There in front of me was a large yellow blob,
And it said to me, 'Hi, my name is Bob.
Would you like to come to my planet for tea?
We will each be eating a giant bogie!'
'No thanks,' I said back to the alien thing,
Then I walked into the darkness and heard a loud ping.
When I turned round it was a wonderful sight,
The alien spaceship was up in mid-flight.
So that night I went home feeling very, very proud,
And told my story to crowd after crowd.

Erin Wainwright (10)
Lent Rise School, Burnham

Bonfire Night

In the night the bonfire glistened,
As the sounds crackled whenever I listened.

The flames were rising up and up,
The people stared and dropped their cup.

The smoke was cloudy and black,
As dark as the night blue sky,
Many people would look over . . . look over to spy.

The fire burning the wood,
The crackling sounds were loud.
You could hardly hear the people, as there was such a crowd.

Whitney Hearn (11)
Lent Rise School, Burnham

Volcanoes Erupting

Clouds of ash are seen in the sky,
It is the volcano erupting,
Lava flows down the outside,
Which is the magma erupting.

Ash, cinders along with other
Materials are also thrown out,
Some lava is thin and runny,
This runs down with speed,
Some lava is thick and sticky,
Creeping forwards slowly.

Destruction is caused by surroundings,
This causes change to the climate,
People's lives completely change,
This is one of the world's biggest natural disasters.

Karisma Uppal (8)
Lent Rise School, Burnham

The Dolphin

The dolphin swam through the open sea,
He splattered and he splashed and he saw a bee,
He said a charming hello,
But the bee just said a horrid goodbye.

The dolphin swam through the open sea,
He splattered and splashed and he saw a colourful flea,
He said a loud hello,
But the flea just said a quiet goodbye.

The dolphin swam through the open sea,
He splattered and he splashed and he saw *me*
He said a sweet hello,
And I said, 'Come and have some apple pie!'

Ayesha Patel (9)
Lent Rise School, Burnham

Winter

Winter's cold
Everything folds,
Trees whooshing,
People pushing.

Skies grey,
Everyday,
Rivers swaying,
Children playing.

Snowman's here,
No more tears,
Snow is falling,
Humans calling.

Rain, but why?
Birds fly,
Everyone's packing,
Bye, bye!

Clair Seymour (10)
Lent Rise School, Burnham

Weather

Wind is calling
Whoosh, whoosh.

Pitter-patter!
Hear the rain,
Leaves are falling
Down, down, down . . .

Winter comes
Cold, cold, days.
Snow is falling.
Don't cry I'm here!
When is it spring?

Bethany Joyce (11)
Lent Rise School, Burnham

The Seasons

In the season of disgraceful weather, winter,
See the snow falling from the sky,
See the flowers as they grow on the rough floor,
In the season of hot and warmness.

Listen to the leaves as they crunch,
Just like a dragon crunching its prey,
In the season of autumn, of which the trees fall.

Watch the trees reappear from their death in spring,
The season in which the sun comes out once again.

With all the seasons,
In one year,
Spring and summer,
Of which the brightness comes out.

Winter and autumn,
The seasons of dull weather.

Daniel Godden (10)
Lent Rise School, Burnham

I Love Sweets

Sweets are delicious,
We want more and more,
Marshmallows are my favourite,
Crunchies, I adore.

My mum says she does not like them,
But she is definitely lying,
She eats them secretly at night,
But she always denies it.

But when I come to think of it,
Vegetables are healthy,
They don't really look like it,
But to pay the dentist bill, I'd have to be wealthy!

Eva Williams (9)
Lent Rise School, Burnham

Guess The Season?

Can you guess some of these?
With snowballs and busy bees,
It might be summer, it might be spring.
You have to guess everything!

Swirling, twirling the leaves are falling.
The wind is blowing and also calling,
The leaves are red with morning mist.
Can you guess which season this is?

The heat is blazing from the smiling sun,
This season is my favourite one,
The bees are buzzing as they whiz,
Can you guess which season this is?

Snowballs flying through the air,
This is a season where we love and care,
This season is cold especially,
Can you guess which season this could be?

Grant Breddy (11)
Lent Rise School, Burnham

The Desert Wasteland

The sand is rich with gold,
Carelessly left there,
The master is alone,
And out of boredom blows his riches,
Seeking a friend,
Frustrated he burns the land,
He shall stay there for eternity,
Bound by an everlasting bond,
What he seeks must come,
Then he shall be free.

Peter Allen (11)
Lent Rise School, Burnham

My Brother

My brother's annoying everyday.
My brother's silly in every way.
My brother's a boy - you can really tell,
Whenever I see him there's an unpleasant smell!

My brother's crazy all the time;
He makes up silly songs that *have* to rhyme!
My brother's stupid when his friends are around,
They all try and make the rudest sound!

My brother thinks he's Superman.
He thinks he's a cartoon like Peter Pan.
My brother really does hate me - but that's OK as I hate him,
like he hates me!

But if my brother wasn't him,
I suppose I might *just* miss him, so really if Matthew wasn't there
I might just realise I love him really and I suppose I do care!

Rachel Evans (11)
Lent Rise School, Burnham

My Favourite Things

Ice cream
Pizza
Chips and nuggets

Oh the joy of hearing children eating,
There's nothing better than a summer's evening,
Hearing the joy of a child's laugh.

No Ice cream
No Pizza,
No chips and nuggets.

Then there is no joy of hearing a child's laugh
And no summer's evening with joyful children.

Kelly Duncan (10)
Lent Rise School, Burnham

My Zoo!

My house is a zoo!
With all my pets I don't know what to do,
Some are big, some are small,
Some shouldn't even be pets at all!

For a start, there's an elephant in the bath,
And the cheetah under the bed,
Well he's a laugh!

There's a monkey in my wardrobe,
There's a lion behind my settee,
A giraffe up my chimney,
He barely notices me!

And the hippo behind the curtain,
He's hard to hide,
The snake in my rabbit hutch,
That's just a guide!

But will my parents ever find out?
I hope not, or I'll know what the punishment will be,
Taking the animals back to the zoo,
And putting me in the cage, too!

Emma Taylor (11)
Lent Rise School, Burnham

Northern Tribes

A rabble from the North,
Painted in black and blue,
Ferocious fire in their eyes,
Spears screaming as they run.

Axes break, swords slash, maces crush
Crush! Crush! Crush!
Merlin leads them, he is wise,
The Wotes are coming, run!

Charlie Lake (11)
Lent Rise School, Burnham

Football

Football, football,
Played at school,
The beers, the cheers,
The evil little sneers.
Watch out for the ball,
The goalkeepers fall,
They went for the kill,
The score is one-nil.

The midfielders attack,
Like a battle in Iraq.
Scoring one more,
And changing the score.
Frustration is here,
For the manager's career,
Is now to end,
The career is taken by his best friend.

Jake Holdstock (11)
Lent Rise School, Burnham

The Cat

The leathery, scaly skin of the cat
Beware as he is wearing a hat
Don't be scared
Just remember it's only a cat

The cats, the cats please run
The cats get away

I can't stand the pace
So I run into space

I see
The big, big
Cat!

Richard Dorrat (10)
Lent Rise School, Burnham

Volcanoes

Volcanoes are boiling,
As hot as the sun.

The lava flows,
Like soft, thick cream.

The lava erupts,
Like shooting stars.

The lava crashes,
As loudly as someone screaming.

The flaming fire,
As dangerous as a dragon.

The flames fly around,
Like flying birds.

The rocks on the volcano,
As hard as steel.

The rocks on the volcano
As bumpy as tree bark.

Neal Sidpara (7)
Lent Rise School, Burnham

Fireworks

F ireworks sizzle in the night,
I see the glitter high in the sky,
R ockets lighting in the night,
E asy to see but not to handle,
W hizzes and whooshes,
O ne time it flashes,
R ed and blue, the colours you see,
K eep away from matches,
S ee the night sparkle and glitter, then it will all end in one big *bang!*

Harriet Johnson (11)
Lent Rise School, Burnham

Final Year

It's my final year at school
I'll have to leave my friends.
I thought my friendships would
Last forever but now they're coming to an end.

I'm nervous about going to a new school
Because I'll have to follow the rules.

I'm scared about my new school uniform
As I'll look silly but everyone is wearing it
So they can't laugh at me.

I'm mostly scared about new friends,
As they might be nice, kind, mean and nasty
But there must be a friend in that school somewhere for me.

My first day is going to be scary, as anything might happen,
Well maybe something scary.
People might joke about my socks
And my locker key might get jammed in the lock.

I'm really going to miss my primary school days,
But something better will come my way.
I will really miss my teachers, my classroom and my friends
But I'll see them again though, one day.

Well that's all about my final year,
So I'll keep worrying until the time's here.

Charlotte Winterflood (10)
Lent Rise School, Burnham

Crashing Waves

The stormy sea, as rough as a carpet ready to come into the shore,
The waves are crashing like they are having a race.
The sea is loud in my ear.
The waves are rising as high as a house.
The sea becomes calm and very smooth,
Ready for the next day to begin.

Molly Colgate (7)
Lent Rise School, Burnham

The Eagle

I swooped over the glossy, white mountains,
As the cold hit my face.
White snow covered the land,
Like a disease spreading through the human body.

My stomach, empty.
As empty as a mind lost in a dreamworld.
I glided lower looking for something to fill my dreamworld
with thoughts.

I saw food.
As fast and determined, I darted through the air.

I attacked,
The prey in my knife like a beak oozed life.
My dreamworld, filled with thoughts,
Beautiful thoughts that filled my mind,
Like water filling the widest ocean.

Stephanie Nathan (10)
Lent Rise School, Burnham

Thunder!

When I strike the rumbling Earth,
All that can be seen is my fiery tail.

Then all that can be heard is my thundering roar,
There is death at every window, at every house.

Suddenly everything is frozen!
And in the distance lights at every house flicker,

And I can hear the leaves rustling in the strong wind,
And the howling screams of young children,

Then suddenly my roar dies down and I can hear,
The hated laughs of young children once again.

Lauren Gillard (11)
Lent Rise School, Burnham

Cars And Their Drivers!

Cars are fast,
As they whiz past,
Some are slow,
Some just blow,
They're not old,
They're just bold,
As they pop along,
Someone's singing a song,
Yeah let's rock,
Bang!
Know they are gone.

It's back,
But it's black,
It's tangled in wire,
And on fire,
The car still moves,
The man still grooves,
It used to zoom,
But not it's boom,
And that's the end of that,
By the way,
He's not going to be back,
Why?
Crash! Bang! Wallop!
That's why.

Oran Brymner (10)
Lent Rise School, Burnham

Snow - Haiku

Snow falls ev'rywhere
People dancing all night long
Christmas is here, now.

Reece Mullins (9)
Lent Rise School, Burnham

A Headless Horseman

One stormy night,
Something light
Rode through our town.

It was on horseback
So I ran out and fed it a tic-tac

The horse didn't like it
So the rider whipped it
And off they galloped, off into the rain

I sat by my window, looking at stars
But all I could see was plenty of cars.

Far out in the lane
I saw he was insane.

The police came up
And bundled them in a truck.

I saw his head
Flaming red.

There was no head
It was a pumpkin.

I jumped into bed
And pulled the covers upon my head.

Savannah Would (9)
Lent Rise School, Burnham

The Desert

The gods blow their glinting golden riches about,
By fluttering gusts,
Sweeping the velvety dunes.
The stars like diamonds lying on a pillow of darkness,
The sun has vanished.
Behind the moon and all of its jewels,
Until dawn, when it will come to be bright once more.

Dylan Calabro (10)
Lent Rise School, Burnham

The Forest Through The Seasons

Trees stand still racing to the sky,
The forest is frequent to passers-by.
Blooming bluebells next to lush green grass,
Sparrows singing but time has passed.

The forest is green, engulfed in sun,
The sky as blue as the sea, looming down on families having fun.
Sunflowers turn their butter, yellow petals high above flowers
and nettles fast,
But the forest knew that summertime was too good to last.

Colours are changing at the speed of lightning,
The tan of trees leaves is really quite frightening,
Sunflowers drooping their usually smiling faces,
Their crispy, brown petals blown to icing lakes.

Frost has fallen and frozen the golden past,
The forest hopes this sadness will be the last.
Rabbits, squirrels hide away,
To return another day.

Now the trees are just large stumps,
Flowers are replaced by litter lumps
Bulldozers come and destroy my being happy
Now the forest is just a memory.

Rebecca Zhao (10)
Lent Rise School, Burnham

Blazing Hot Volcanoes

Volcanoes are hot as the sun
Volcanoes are as drippy as fountains
They explode like rockets.
And shoot into the sky like a star
They're rocky as an old roof
Bubbling like shampoo
Dangerous as blazing fire
Flames orange, red and yellow
Very impressive you know.

Emily Nurcombe (7)
Lent Rise School, Burnham

People's Feelings Change

Everyone prefers someone to another and can make this very clear,
They also know people who make them gather fear.
People's emotions change as they see different views,
Some make them sad, some sad and some angry too.

You cannot change emotions, as they come straight from the heart,
They can change your way in life and that comes from
when you start.
Emotions will always change through childhood and adulthood,
So we can't change that, even if you think we should.

Christopher Organ (10)
Lent Rise School, Burnham

Dolphins

Dolphins swim in any sea
Any sea with me, me, me.
When they flip up to the sky,
I feel like a butterfly.
Dolphins swim in any sea
Any sea with me, me, me.

Laura New (11)
Lent Rise School, Burnham

Winter's Secrets

Winter has lots of secrets,
Some in peculiar places,
But I'm not going to blow their cover,
They're out there, for you to discover.

Nicolas Szwenk (10)
Lent Rise School, Burnham

Boiling Volcanoes

The boiling volcanoes are very hot
Beware of the lava
The boiling volcanoes are full of lava
Because volcanoes need lava
The hot air comes out of the volcanoes
And shoots up and up
The bubbling volcanoes are hot
They are hotter than an iron
The exploding lava out from the volcanoes
Shoots fast up into the air
The rocky volcanoes are rough as a
Tree bark
The lava is sprayed everywhere
It is like an earthquake
So be careful
You must be careful more than anything
Because of the boiling volcanoes.

Faine Slattery (7)
Lent Rise School, Burnham

My Guinea Pig

My guinea pig is sweet,
When she squeaks,
She has a small pink nose,
And sneezes like a hose.

My guinea pig is as gentle as a fly,
When she whines for my food.
She gnaws at the bars on her cage,
And she is rather beige.

Charlie-Freya Keates (10)
Lent Rise School, Burnham

Weather

There are all different types of weather.
Weather we like,
Weather we don't like.
I know the weather I like.

My favourite weather is when it's sunny.
The acres of grassy fields,
The trees blow around, as the sun shines upon them,
When it's sunny, it's a time for fun.
Sunny weather is the best.

I also like it when it snows.
Children playing, children having fun,
Making snowmen and throwing snowballs,
As the snow falls upon them,
Snowy weather is wonderful.

The weather we don't like is the thunder and rain.
Rain gives you a sad feeling,
When everyone is inside, hiding from the weather.
With thunder we all run and scream,
As it strikes and hits our world,
Thunder and rain is a real pain.

The worst weather ever is a tornado.
Its whirly wind destroys our land,
It knocks over houses, cars, you name it, its gone,
It leaves people crying, that's not fair.
Tornados are the worst.

James Hirst (11)
Lent Rise School, Burnham

My Pets

I love my dog because it is fun to play with.
I love my cat because it loves me so much.
I love my rabbit because it eats all of its food.
I like my pig because it chases me all day.
I have a mouse in my house and it takes my cheese.

Toni Harding (8)
Lent Rise School, Burnham

Volcanoes

Volcanoes are flowing with fear,
They are dangerous for exploding.
Volcanoes have blazing lava,
As hot as the sun.

The flames of lava,
Are like fountains.
Volcanoes are impressive,
Because they are blazing with bubbles.

They are flashing with excitement,
Inside is dazzling with glowing fires.
Volcanoes disturb neighbouring villages,
And destroy useful land.

Once lava has dried up,
It turns into molten rock.
Volcanoes erupt quickly,
As fast as Kelly Holmes!

Abigail Jones (7)
Lent Rise School, Burnham

Fireworks, Fireworks

Fireworks, fireworks in the night,
All the colours are shining bright.

Fireworks, fireworks you're all around,
Then you make such a sound.

Fireworks, fireworks so delight
I think of you through the night.

Fireworks, fireworks, it's coming to an end
I've had such fun with my friend.

Monique Wilkes (11)
Lent Rise School, Burnham

Volcanoes

Volcanoes erupt, fountains of lava spray
First a menacing rumble shatters everything
The rumble is like an earthquake
Dark ash clouds block the sunlight
Volcanoes erupt.

Lava is sprayed rapidly
Orange goo flows from the top
Everything is perished that stands in its way.

Volcanoes erupt
Molten rock that settles for a thousand years explodes
Volcanoes erupt
Lava is sprayed from the highest peak
Volcanoes erupt.
Beware!

Aaron Yeung (8)
Lent Rise School, Burnham

The Beast Of The Water

Crash goes the claws of the raging beast,
Smash goes the nails of this gruesome beast,
Green as a frog, sharp as a knife,
Lashing out to passers-by.

Huge fangs sprout out of the water,
Crashing into boats and sending splinters everywhere.
Beware; do not go out onto this wretched water,
Because this beast is the peril of the ocean.

So never go too far from the beach,
Never,
Never,
Or you'll have a scary time with this horrible beast.

Samuel Leech (8)
Lent Rise School, Burnham

Volcanoes

Volcanoes bursting to erupt
Lava travelling down and down!
Volcanoes blazing hot.
Lava boiling, rocky and fast.

In a few hundred years a volcano erupts
Stones spitting out like shooting stars.
People in houses will not get warned.
You will not have a chance to run from the blazing lava.

The red lava will get you even if you run.

Ruby Blackley (7)
Lent Rise School, Burnham

Crazy Football

There's a monkey on the left wing,
A cheetah on the right,
But watch out for Nelly the Elephant,
She might give you a bit of a fright.

There's a leopard in defence,
A tiger in midfield,
But you know Gilly the Giraffe in goal,
A hippo would be a better shield.

But with Roger the Rhino as referee
You can't get away with anything.
And as soon as Ronald the Rat comes on,
He gets squashed by the ball, whilst starting to sing!

Rebecca Maul (11)
Lent Rise School, Burnham

Volcano

Volcano flowing like thick cream,
Trickles down the mountain like syrup,
Burning all the houses,
Running down the street,
Chasing all the people.

The volcano still spurting out hot lava,
Roaring like a lion,
Escaping from the top,
Circling round the mountain,
Splitting the mountain at the top,
Bits of ash falling off,
Into the burning lava below.

Matthew Anderson (7)
Lent Rise School, Burnham

Vibrating Volcanoes

Volcanoes are as hot as the burning sun.
Bubbling like a bubble bath, waiting to be bathed in.
Patiently waiting to erupt.
Ten, nine, eight, seven, six, five, four, three,
Two, one, zero.
Erupt!
Spilling down like golden syrup.
Mixing in with the molten rock.
Destroying everything that tries to stop it.
Some people think it's never going to stop.
Vibrating volcanoes kill.

Madeline Wallace (8)
Lent Rise School, Burnham

Volcanoes That Erupt

Lava travels down a volcano fast,
Exploding at the very top,
Boiling, bubbling inside it
Hotter than two thousand degrees
Blazing from holes all over it.

Lava travels quickly down
Shooting from the highest peak,
Rumbling, bumbling inside it,
Nearly as hot as the sun,
Jumping from holes all over it.

Lava travels bubbling all the way down,
Blowing at the very top,
Boiling, bubbling inside it,
As hot as flames from fire,
Erupting from holes all over it.

Peter Moriarty (7)
Lent Rise School, Burnham

Two Terrific Tortoises

One wonderful wardrobe,
Two terrific tortoises,
Three free fish,
Four fun fishermen,
Five friendly females,
Six silly snakes,
Seven safe storms,
Eight enormous eels,
Nine naughty knights,
Ten told tales.

Daisy Hodghton (8)
Lent Rise School, Burnham

Lava, Lava

Watch out! Here it goes
The big volcano explodes.
Hot ashes coming out,
Everybody screams and shouts.
Hot ashes going everywhere,
On the floor and in the air.
Molten lava spreading,
Travelling down the stem of the volcano.

Rumbling and bumbling,
Flowing along the paths of the village,
A lava monster swims in the lava-like stream.

Look it's getting up
I think he is going to *eat me!*

Daniel Martin (7)
Lent Rise School, Burnham

Rising Volcanoes

Rising volcanoes are boiling hot,
They are rocky too,
Rocks start to shoot very high,
The lava comes down very fast.

Inside the volcano, very bubbly
It's as bubbly as a bath
Outside the volcano it's very bumpy
It's as bumpy as a rock.

The lava is like cream
Cream is very soft
Dark ash covers the sky
The volcano is about to erupt.

Sara Maltempi (8)
Lent Rise School, Burnham

The Volcano

Run, run
Everyone,
It's the volcano
It's erupting.

See the
Red stuff
Falling down
The hill.
It's lava
Argh!

The flying
Rock coming
Out of
The top
Like tiny
Little
Meteors.

Disturbing
All the babies
Sleeping very
Calmly
Waah, waah.

Jake MacNaughton (8)
Lent Rise School, Burnham

Volcano

The volcano is as hot as the sun.
The volcano is as bubbly, as bubbly soap.
The volcano looks like a fountain, when it erupts.
The volcano is dangerous when it is about to explode
onto the molten rock.
The flames are blazing like the sun.
The volcano shoots down the slope very fast.

Sarah Cartmell (7)
Lent Rise School, Burnham

Volcanoes

Volcanoes are boiling and loud
Volcanoes are hot and growling
Volcanoes are dark and shooting
Getting hotter and hotter
About to explode fire
About to shoot
About to burst like a big balloon
Rising higher and higher
About to blow up the whole earth
Exploding lava spills over the sides
People are about to have the last day of their lives!

Emily Hicks (7)
Lent Rise School, Burnham

Volcanoes

Lava goes as high as the clouds
It is as boiling as the sun,
It erupts like a shooting star
It slithers slowly down the volcano like a snail.
It is as thick as ice cream
It is amazing, as if a miracle was performed.

Conn O'Brien (7)
Lent Rise School, Burnham

Volcanoes

Volcanoes erupt hot and loud
Shooting fast like a star.

Blazing like fire, dangerous as dragons
Exploding with bubbles,
Pop, pop, pop they're all gone!

Harvin Chohan (7)
Lent Rise School, Burnham

Cats

Cats are nice
Some are not nice
Some cats are horrible
Some cats are not horrible
Some cats are sleepy
Some cats are lazy
Some cats are not sleepy,
Some cats are not lazy,
Cats come out at night
And dance around with the other cats.
Some cats don't come out and dance around with other cats.
Because they have to go inside for their dinner
But they cannot go back outside again.
Do you have a cat?
If you do and it has kittens they might be the same.

Drew Collman (7)
Lent Rise School, Burnham

Storm Island

At the beach the waves are clashing
The waves were high like a tidal wave.
The dark clouds covered the light of the sun.

The waves were bigger,
Then there was a loud crash,
It was the clashing, bashing, splashing of the waves,
Swinging the waves against the sand.

All was dark, like the clouds.
Waves were angry and charging,
Washing the rocks and sand off the shore.
That is the end of the storm of Storm Island.

Kalem Randhawa (8)
Lent Rise School, Burnham

Teachers Are Great

T eachers always say, 'Detention! Detention! Detention!'
E mma, Savannah, Kristine, stand to attention,
A ll they want for Christmas is chocolate and wine,
C hildren think they're fab and fine,
H orrible teachers, always there,
E gg the car! And . . .
R un! Run! Get out of here!
S tudents always peer and don't forget they're always here!

A lways mean
R arely clean
E veryday teachers run away!

G reat teachers, sometimes cool
R arely never come to school because they're always at the pool.
E veryday, something strange happens to them,
A teacher is tall and sometimes will fall,
T he best teachers ever are Miss Long and Mr Greasley!

Hannah Slade (9)
Lent Rise School, Burnham

Underwater

Under the water in the deep blue sea,
There are lots of fishes that you can see.
There are weird crabs, colourful clown fishes and maybe a shark.
There is also a shipwreck called the 'Matty Lark'.
There are reds and blues and oranges and grey,
There are actually more colours than I could ever say,
The seabed is covered in coral reefs,
Then humans came along and took some fish, just like a thief.

Samuel Burnham (10)
Lent Rise School, Burnham

Dragons

Bumpy scales, golden spikes
Fiery flames burn the toast that he likes;
On his body not a flea,
His teeth as big as a tall tree.

The body so colourful
The body so wonderful,
Moving swiftly to catch his prey
Gulping down his food as he lay.

On his black body, golden dots,
The spikes on his back as big as pots,
His tongue's long like a fork,
But he doesn't eat pork.

Dragons are wonderful creatures
Although I would not like to meet them.

Rhianna Mohindru (9)
Lent Rise School, Burnham

Volcanoes Erupting

Volcanoes erupting down the rocky hills,
Don't touch it; it's too hot,
Blazing lava shooting everywhere,
Going down the mountains.

It's like dark, hot, boiling, bubbly ash,
It travels as fast as light.
Dangerous fire on the Rocky Mountains
Wow, impressive, amazing volcanoes are erupting.

It's destroying all the green grass and trees,
It reaches the village
And people are running all over the place
Wow, wow the volcanoes are erupting.

Abigail Hirst (8)
Lent Rise School, Burnham

My Puppy Fleur!

My puppy Fleur
Never does purr
She's really really cute
And never does hoot
She's a Border collie
She loves it on my boat, Folly.

She's got a beauty spot
She runs around and gets hot
Her real name's Flower
She has the power.

She's a lot of fun
She'll eat a hot cross bun
She's got cute brown eyes
That reflect the skies

My puppy Fleur!

Hannah Swallow (9)
Lent Rise School, Burnham

Wondrous World

The world is wondrous
The plants, the animals and their tails like a brush
Uluru, Sahara and the oil
How those deserts make you boil!
Many creatures live in the sea
I wish one of them could be me!
Further down we still don't know
It's better kept a secret though,
We've added more, like the car and the bus
How the world is wondrous.

Adam Harmsworth (10)
Lent Rise School, Burnham

The Sound

I hear a calm piece of music,
It runs into my ears,
I see myself on a boat,
The water glistening around me,
The sun shining its yellow rays
The sky clear and blue
The sea creatures dancing
The dolphins swim gracefully,
The whales squirt water
Colourful, tropical fish jumping in the air
Seals waving their tails,
Seagulls flying in the air,
Waves crashing against the rocks
Sharks leading the boat to the Caribbean
I lay there
Dazzled by this moment,
I wish life was like this.

Clare Shepherd (10)
Lent Rise School, Burnham

Shark!

Scuba-diving in the deep blue sea,
I think that something is following me,
Something that is very long,
Even longer than King Kong,
Its teeth are sharp,
Its fins are grey,
I wish that I could swim away
This creature isn't scared of the dark,
Because this creature is a shark!

Emma Cottenham (9)
Lent Rise School, Burnham

Fire Spirit

Flowing, glowing, disturbing,
It is coming, shooting, bubbling, and molten
He is breaking through his prison.
Boiling, impressive, fast he is using his ultimate weapon.
Rising out, growing stronger, his danger's growing more powerful,
Only one weakness, more of it than him.
Skin bubbling and he sleeps for a long time,
Then awakens from his prison and destroys life from miles around.
Now free from his prison
We can tell you his name and he is called the Fire Spirit
And he only does one thing, destroy.

James Burgess (8)
Lent Rise School, Burnham

Cats

Cats can climb anything.
Cats can climb on pipes.
Cats can climb on lights.
Cats can climb on beds.
Cats can climb on sheds.
Cats can climb on mice.
Cats can climb on ice.
Cats can climb on bikes.
Cats can climb on trikes.
Cats can climb up trees.
Cats can climb on knees.
Cats can climb up clocks.
Cats can climb in boxes.
Cats can climb up houses.
Cats can climb on trousers.
Cats can climb on dads.
Cats can climb on crabs.
Cats can climb anything.

Eoghan Perkins (8)
Lismore Primary School, Oban

Animals

Dogs bark.

Dogs bark at rabbits
Dogs bark at you
Dogs bark at people
Dogs bark at cars
Dogs bark at cats.

Dogs bark

Bears growl

Bears growl at bears
Bears growl at people
Bears growl at birds
Bears growl at mirrors
Bears growl at grass

Bears growl

Lions roar

Lions roar at tigers
Lions roar at fences
Lions roar at grass
Lions roar at dogs
Lions roar at trees

Lions roar.

Fiona MacLean (9)
Lismore Primary School, Oban

Rally

Rallies, rallies losing wheels
Metal, metal smashing cars
Hairpin corners of the track
To get to the end of the rally
Cars are skidding on the tracks
Ford, Citroen, all kinds of cars
To get to the end of the rally
Drivers, drivers risking death
To win at the end of the rally.

Colin Black (10)
Lismore Primary School, Oban

Orienteering

Orienteering is so fun,
Look for the symbols,
Run, run, run.
Racing round the curvy bend,
There's a symbol stuck to the wall,
I reach; it's way up tall,
I copy it down to my paper,
I'll show it to Miss . . . later!
Racing round the climbing frame,
People have finished,
What a shame!
I like orienteering,
It's really fun,
With my friends,
Here I come,
I'm nearly finished,
Only one more,
There it is,
On the door,
I copy it down to my paper,
Then I'll show it to Miss . . . later!

Chloe Walton (10)
Marpool Primary School, Exmouth

A Bit Over The Top

When I went orienteering,
I went over the top
I went over the hills,
But would not stop!
I don't like English, science or maths,
So I decided to take the orienteering paths.

The smell was minging
With cow poo and horse poo!
So instead of singing,
I was full of remorse.
Then I thought, *what should I do?*
I really, badly needed the loo!

I must be crazy,
With my brain like a pea,
But I won't be lazy,
Because that's not me!

When I was done,
I ran down the hill.
Just like Jack
From Jack and Jill,
When I was home
I lay on my bed,
While I was lying,
My legs felt dead!
My mum came in the room and said,
'It's time for school,
Get out of bed!'

Francis Marshall (10)
Marpool Primary School, Exmouth

Terrible Tudors

They were terrible; Tudors,
In a terrible time,
And if you are squeamish,
Skip this rhyme.

Arthur, the favourite,
I'm afraid he died.
Henry, the other,
Well, he survived.
Henry grew older,
And as fat as a bear,
He married six wives,
And had three new heirs.
Mary, the oldest
Was a young catholic,
Ed was protestant,
But weak and sick.
Elizabeth was neither,
Did not join in fights
But killed all offenders,
That came in her sight.
Together the family,
Killed all that they could,
Beheaded or burnt,
Bad people or good.

If you want to argue,
I suggest that you stop
If you argue with Tudors,
You're for the *chop!*

Bethany Foxon (11)
Marpool Primary School, Exmouth

Henry The Eighth

Henry the Eighth, oh Henry the Eighth.
He had too much upon his plate,
He had six wives and he was fat,
And wore a feather in his hat!

He was desperate for a son,
He thought it would be lots of fun,
He'd be the right man for the throne,
Henry would teach him till he'd grown.

Henry would love his growing boy,
Give him arrows for his toys,
Weapons, daggers and then swords,
So his son would not get bored.

Henry the eighth, oh Henry the Eighth
He had too much upon his plate,
In Tudor times you would be dead,
Henry would cut off your *head!*

Jessica Dommett (9)
Marpool Primary School, Exmouth

Magic Garden

Fog is clearing can't you see
Trees are blossoming in the spring
The pond is flowing like a waterfall
Flowers are opening like a fairy's wings.

Birds are tweeting like a flute
Wind is blowing like a puff
The little pixies dancing all round

The acorns dropping on the ground
The little ginger squirrels running all round

The door opening to the world
Leaves are swaying.

This is a world of magic.

Emma Morgan (9)
Marpool Primary School, Exmouth

School

I went into school,
They had a new rule,
We are allowed to bring toys,
And we are allowed to chase the boys.

We like to be cool,
Definitely in a pool.
There is glass on the floor,
Right near the door.

When the girls,
Wear loads of pearls,
If the teacher is away,
You may have to pay.

If this day,
Is May,
Would you go there?
Because it is very rare.

Kayley Shepherd (9)
Marpool Primary School, Exmouth

Gymnastics

I go to gymnastics
It's on every Wednesday,
We go to competitions,
And you don't have to pay!

You have to do a warm up,
Before you start,
Stretch your legs,
And increase the beat of your heart.

I can do a lot of moves,
From rolls to handsprings,
I can do things on the vault,
It's like you've got wings.

Amy Prowse (10)
Marpool Primary School, Exmouth

Lauren

Her hair is as orange as a ripe tangerine,
Her eyes are as blue as the rippling sea,
She likes the colour, dark green,
But she hates a cup of tea.

Her skin is as soft as a newborn puppy,
She swims as fast as a silver guppy,
She does not eat meat,
She likes to stay in the heat.

Her voice flows like 1,000 butterflies,
She is as jolly as a row of hot pies,
She is as nice as a dancing flower,
She has a lot of power.

She's like a bird, soaring through the sky,
She's as playful as a tiger cub,
I know that to me she will never lie,
We are best friends, Lauren and I.

Shannon Brown (10)
Marpool Primary School, Exmouth

School

S chool is where people make a friend or two
C ould be me or it could be you
H unting for things for orienteering in PE
O r doing dance inside, so no one can see!
O n the playground would be a good place to start
L earning and being taught is the worst part.

Anya Evans (11)
Marpool Primary School, Exmouth

Shannon

Her hair is like petals on a sunflower
Her eyes remind me of smooth, dark chocolate
Her skin is as soft as a feather.
Her voice is like birds singing.

Her feet are as small as a mouse,
Her heart is as big as the world,
Her thoughts are for all around,
Kindness she shares with everyone.

She's as fragile as a butterfly,
She's as soft as a marshmallow
She's as sweet as treacle pudding
She's kind and caring and always sharing.

Her smile is for all to see,
She is my best friend; Shannon.

Lauren Williams (10)
Marpool Primary School, Exmouth

Camping

Summer camping
Happy and fun
Smells of nature
Sounds of birds

Stormy and wet,
Biting mosquitoes,
Freezing toast,
Soggy clothes.

Happy and sad times,
But will miss the fun,
We've go to go,
We're driving home.

Roxanne Newberry (11)
Marpool Primary School, Exmouth

Henry VIII's Wives

Catherine of Aragon,
Was the first to come,
She was divorced,
Time to move on.

Anne Boleyn,
Only three years
She was beheaded,
It put Henry in tears.

Jane Seymour,
Had an illness so bad,
Deserved to live,
But Henry was sad.

Anne of Cleaves,
Gosh, five months,
Another divorce
She was down in the dumps.

Catherine Howard
That flirty old girl,
Her head was shot off,
Like a shooting hurl.

Catherine Parr
Was sweetie pie,
It was Henry's turn,
He was to die.

The Tudors were terrible,
Now you know,
My poem is finished,
It is my turn to go!

Rhiannon Kirk (11)
Marpool Primary School, Exmouth

The Universe

U p in space there rests a place
N ever does it move or sleep
I n the murky blackness
V enus, Neptune all the planets
E ngulfed in black and loads of stars
R oaming asteroids deadly comets
S tars glittering like diamond jewels
E xtremely big, the universe.

George Bennett (10)
Marpool Primary School, Exmouth

This Cage Holds Greatness

He's great
He's got fire for hair,
Smells of brilliant aftershave,
Bite him and you will drown,
He has a cool laugh,
Touch him and you will be electrocuted
You will find him in a biscuit tin.

Robert Noonan (9)
Murray's Road Junior School, Douglas

There Was An Old Man From Poole

There was an old man from Poole
Who thought he was very cool
He fell off his bike
So started to hike
That weird old man from Poole.

Charlotte Harcourt (10)
Murray's Road Junior School, Douglas

My Brother

He is a soft bed,
He's a ruby-red diamond which is always gleaming,
He's a purring cat,
A handsome black crow,
The smell of a petrol station,
The sound of a dolphin calling to its mother,
A lovely sunset with a hot bath,
A bottle of Coca-Cola
A bricklayer.

Katie Devereau (10)
Murray's Road Junior School, Douglas

My Friend Ka U Lam

She's a soft squishy bed,
She's a bright yellow sun always shining,
She's a brown and white bouncy bunny,
A white dove flying to the moon,
The smell of a purple violet,
The happy sounds of birds singing,
A fresh sunny morning with lovely sunflowers,
A tasty chocolate smoothie,
An angel.

Natasha Johnson (9)
Murray's Road Junior School, Douglas

There Was A Boy Called Josh

There was a boy called Josh,
Who never had a wash,
He fell down a well,
And started to smell,
That crazy boy called Josh.

Joshua Brand (10)
Murray's Road Junior School, Douglas

Night

Night is kind and caring,
She makes me feel relaxed and calm,
Her face looks tanned and shiny,
Her eyes are sparkling light blue,
Her mouth is like a moon,
Her hair is soft, long and blonde,
Her clothes are made of cotton,
When she moves she sparkles,
She speaks softly and calmly,
She lives in the sky with friends and enemies,
Night and I are friends.

Kim O'Driscoll (11)
Murray's Road Junior School, Douglas

My Friend

She's a new, soft, squishy couch
She's a yellow sun always there for me
She's a purring, pretty, funny cat
A fast pigeon flying to the moon
The smell of a summer rose
The sound of a weird and unusual ring-tone on a phone
A freaky Friday watching scary films
A fizzy glass of Cherry Coke
A spy.

Sarah Woods (10)
Murray's Road Junior School, Douglas

My Mum

My mum is sweet
My mum is kind
My mum never leaves me behind
My mum is beautiful and she's just fine.

Rebecca Callister (9)
Murray's Road Junior School, Douglas

Why?

'I'm just going out for a moment.'
'Why?'
'Because I'm thirsty.'
'Why?'
'Because it's sunny.'
'Why?'
'Because it's summer.'
'Why?'
'Because it's the summer season.'
'Why?'
'Because that's when it is.'
'Why?'
'High time you stop saying why all the time.'
'What!'

Emily Murphy (7)
Murray's Road Junior School, Douglas

The Night Sky

Night is a kind and caring person,
She makes me feel gentle,
Her face looks like the night sky,
Her eyes are stars,
Her mouth is a white, wispy cloud,
Her hair is long and blonde,
She wears a silky, red ballroom dress,
She moves very swiftly,
She speaks quietly,
She lives in a big white mansion with a huge garden,
Night relaxes me and is my friend.

Heather McMahon (11)
Murray's Road Junior School, Douglas

My Friend Hannah

She's a soft, red sofa with new cushions,
She's a cool, light blue swimming pool,
She's a bouncy grey whale,
A white dove soaring over each cloud it sees,
A yellow sunflower always shining,
The sound of a new McFly sound each day!
A midnight feast!
A fizzy cup of lemonade.

Chloë Shimmin (10)
Murray's Road Junior School, Douglas

My Pets

My snake slithers, slithers, slithers.
My horse neighs, neighs, neighs.
My rabbit crunches, crunches, crunches.
My frog ribbits, ribbits, ribbits.
My dolphin squeaks, squeaks, squeaks.
My shark snaps, snaps, snaps.
My fish swims, swims, swims.
My turtle hides, hides, hides
And my cat naps all day long.

Emily Bray (9)
Murray's Road Junior School, Douglas

Scrappy

Scrappy is cute
Scrappy is furry
Scrappy is nice
Scrappy is curly.
Guess what he is?
He is my dog.

Charlotte Percival (9)
Murray's Road Junior School, Douglas

Night

Night is a kind angel who loves all,
He makes me feel so good,
His face is like a star,
His eyes are like suns,
His mouth is like a half-moon,
His hair is made of gold,
His clothes are made of silk,
He moves like a mouse, so fast and so quiet,
When he speaks the birds sing,
He lives in a cloud with angels and birds,
Night saves me.

Jake Corkish (11)
Murray's Road Junior School, Douglas

Sound

Stars glimmering in the night,
The sun shining in your eyes,
The moon's reflection in the pond,
The clouds floating in the sky,
The owls sleeping on a branch,
The birds whistle in your ears,
What can you hear?

Emma Carus (11)
Murray's Road Junior School, Douglas

Anger

Anger is sapphire blue, like coldness.
Anger feels like ice.
Anger smells like mint.
Anger tastes like ice and strong mints.
Anger sounds like strong waves of water.

James Collister (8)
Murray's Road Junior School, Douglas

Outside!

Outside, outside,
Skateboards on the playground floor,
People strolling,
Oh outside, the best of all.

Outside, outside,
People chatting at the door,
Girls are giggling,
Boys are sniggering,
Oh, the outside world.

Rebecca Johnson (9)
Murray's Road Junior School, Douglas

Death

This cage holds death,
I am Death.
I am a black cloak,
I smell of dead bodies over one hundred years old,
I taste of blood which is fresh,
I sound of deathly screams and feel stuffy air,
I live in the oldest gravestone in the darkest corner of the graveyard.

Callum Trenholme (9)
Murray's Road Junior School, Douglas

Playtime

Playtime is a time to play.
Playtime is three times a day.
Playtime is when you fall out.
Playtime is when you hang about.
Playtime is when you spin around.
Playtime is when you fall on the ground.

Juan Riordan (8)
Murray's Road Junior School, Douglas

Anger

Anger is a feeling when you are mad.
It feels like you are on fire.
Anger smells stinky and smelly.
Anger tastes like a hot bubbly sweet.
Anger sounds like hot bubbly fire.

Philippa Kennaugh (7)
Murray's Road Junior School, Douglas

Question And Answer Poem!

What is love?
A happy, joyful feeling.
What is hatred?
An angry, spiteful feeling.
What is hope?
A dream, a wish, a fantasy.
What is sadness?
An upset, hurt feeling.
What is joy?
A happy, glad feeling.
What is calmness?
A still, relaxed feeling.

Becky Lampitt (10)
Murray's Road Junior School, Douglas

Loneliness

Loneliness is blue like the cold, salty sea,
Loneliness feels like boring old tools,
Loneliness smells like bored old bees,
Loneliness tastes like cold ice-cubes,
Loneliness sounds like a chuffing train.

Emily Brennan (8)
Murray's Road Junior School, Douglas

Why?

'I'm going to the chippy.'
'Why?'
'Because I'm hungry.'
'Why?'
'Because it is lunchtime.'
'Why?'
'Because . . .'
'Why?'
'Because I'm hungry and it is lunchtime.'
'Why?'
'Can you please stop saying why.'
'Why?'
'Because I said so!'
'What!'

Mia Sultana (8)
Murray's Road Junior School, Douglas

Sweet Little Girls

Sweet little girls,
Always wear pearls.

They wear pretty dresses
And never make messes.

They have beautiful hair,
Which is very fair.

They dance beautifully,
And practise it very carefully.

Their hair goes bright in the light,
Oh I wish every girl was sweet.

Sophie Cuthbert (9)
Murray's Road Junior School, Douglas

Flowers

I like flowers,
Roses, buttercups, lilies,
Sweet smelling flowers.
People who don't like flowers
Are silly billys!

Jemima Morrow (9)
Murray's Road Junior School, Douglas

Thank You For Everything

Thank you for the sun and rain
Thank you for my friends
Thank you for the animals and things
But thank you for everything.

Emily Rimmer (7)
Murray's Road Junior School, Douglas

Fairies

Fairies flutter in the sky
They flutter so, so very high.
The fairies hover to say goodbye
Because they like to flutter in the sky.

Alisha Taubman (8)
Murray's Road Junior School, Douglas

Scooters

I'm desperate for a scooter
I'll go very fast,
Whizzing up and down the path.

Laura Pover (7)
Murray's Road Junior School, Douglas

Boredom

Boredom is pink, like the bud of a new rose,
Boredom feels lifeless, glum,
Dungeoned like Rapunzel.
Boredom smells of smelly socks
Of a toilet not cleaned out.
Boredom tastes of mouldy chips,
Like an untouched egg.
Boredom sounds of a dreadful singer.

Siobhan Fuller (7)
Murray's Road Junior School, Douglas

Anger

Anger is like burning chillies,
Anger is like fighting temper,
Anger is very hard to fight,
Anger is very bad when you're mad,
Anger is very painful,
Anger can make you explode,
Anger is very difficult to fight,
Anger is very stressful.

Sam Greasley (8)
Murray's Road Junior School, Douglas

Hope

Hope is a white diamond that sparkles bright,
It smells like spring flowers,
Hope tastes like spring,
It sounds like birds tweeting,
Hope feels smooth and soft,
It lives inside your little heart.

Breeshey Cowin (9)
Murray's Road Junior School, Douglas

The Blazing Sun

The sun brightens my day when I awake,
Sparkling through my curtains.
It makes me full of joy and warm inside.
When I'm lying on the beach, it makes my pale skin brown.
But warming, the sun can also burn your skin,
So always wear sun cream!

Katherine Blenkinsop (8)
Murray's Road Junior School, Douglas

Colours

Red stands for a juicy apple.
Orange stands for a springy ball.
Yellow stands for the shining sun.
Blue stands for the sparkly sea.
Green stands for the wavy grass.
Red, orange, yellow, blue and green
Stand for the colourful rainbow!

Fay Wilcox & Eva Boyd (7)
Murray's Road Junior School, Douglas

Happiness

Happiness is blue like the sky,
Happiness feels like cold ice-cubes,
Happiness smells like colourful flowers,
Happiness tastes like the red bright roses,
Happiness sounds like happy, smiley, funny children.

Caitlin Cowin (7)
Murray's Road Junior School, Douglas

The Freaky Troll!

Be wary of the hairy troll,
That patiently lies in wait,
To drag you to his dingy hole,
And put you on his plate!

His blood is green and burning hot,
He gurgles, gobbles and groans,
He'll stir you in his dinner pot,
Your skin, your flesh, your bones!

He'll stretch your arms,
And break your legs,
And grind you to a pulp,
Then swallow you up like a slimy slug,
Crunch! Munch! Gulp!

So watch your step next time you go,
Upon a stinky stroll,
Or you might end up in the pit below
As breakfast for the troll!

Hannah Riordan (10)
Murray's Road Junior School, Douglas

Hallowe'en

I like Hallowe'en
It's a lovely scene.
People are walking around,
Creepy things on the ground.
A haunted house,
Find that mouse.
Look at that big heap,
It looks like a scared sheep.
Look at the moon's beam,
A witch's shadow can be seen.

Emily Hoare (11)
Musbury Primary School, Axminster

Last Night

Last night as I walked my dog
Through a place I've never been before,
Standing in front of me was a great big metal door,
I looked up and saw as dark as night, but crystal clear,
A great big mansion as far as the pier,
As I stepped through the door,
I began to wonder more and more,
When I stepped forward the hairs on my arm stuck up on end,
I started to wish I had a comforting friend.

Stephanie Allen (10)
Musbury Primary School, Axminster

Talking On A Tooth

'Yuck! It's drinking the healthy stuff.'
'Oh, yum here comes the red stuff, very sweet stuff.'
'How come you get fatty stuff?'
'Yours is on diet stuff.'
'How do you know that stuff?'
'I actually hear stuff.'
'You're very lucky.'
'Ah well, here comes the string stuff.'
Oh! Bye! Germ!

Stephanie Herbert (9)
Musbury Primary School, Axminster

Christmas Trees

Frozen water just like shiny ice,
Woolly jumpers on freezing people,
White cold snow, like sprinkling snowflakes,
Shimmering Christmas trees near brown sledges,
Sparkling decorations with colourful presents underneath.

Alice Gay (9)
Musbury Primary School, Axminster

Free

I don't have to worry about bullies,
They used to hide up trees,
They used to stand by the trees whispering,
They used to punch me,
They picked on me,
I was in a cold place,
I shouted for help and no one answered.

Then suddenly a boy came,
He grabbed them,
They didn't like it,
They legged it.

We became best friends,
I don't have to worry about bullies
Anymore.

Laurence Gay (8)
Musbury Primary School, Axminster

Steph

S teph is as sweet as a rose.
T all and pretty.
E arly blossoming.
P retty brown eyes and brown hair.
H oping for someone to pick her some day.

Kaya Williams (9)
Musbury Primary School, Axminster

Rudolph The Red-Nosed Reindeer

Rudolph you have a shiny nose
I wish I could see it because it glows.
And if I don't see it, I won't know how it goes.
I do believe in Christmas but I want to see you.

Jaymie Glover (8)
Musbury Primary School, Axminster

Bullying

Shouting,
Screaming,
Running across the road,
I don't know what to do,
I have to run,
I'm puffing like crazy,
I really hate you,
Leave me alone, don't hurt me,
Leave me alone, I want to be free.

Jessica Rowden (9)
Musbury Primary School, Axminster

The Sea

As I run so fast,
My feet are hot,
Running, breathless, legs so tired
Falling down to the sand,
The sea so cold, the sun so hot,
I'm feeling anxious, feeling cold
Because I'm scared and wet.

Rosa Hanley (10)
Musbury Primary School, Axminster

Help

Walking,
Running,
Stumbling,
Falling,
Trying to hide,
Too late,
Bleeding.

Lauren Ellis (10)
Musbury Primary School, Axminster

Tummy Tantrums

The stomach is all clean,
The breath is all a bliss,
The body is all healthy,
But I'll soon change this.

How can you complain?
When my life is all at risk,
'Cause the paranoid giants
Wash me in a large round disk.

At least you don't have medicine,
Chasing you all around.
Then I've got to hide,
And hope that I'm not found.

Oh no, it's moving to a bathroom,
And a large round disk is coming to view,
Here comes the end of my life,
So goodbye to you.

Danielle Herbert (11)
Musbury Primary School, Axminster

Who Am I?

I have fur as white as snow,
What am I?
I have two little things on my head,
What am I?
I have a little thing on my behind,
What am I?
I live in a cage,
What am I?
If you haven't guessed yet,
Well I'm a . . .
Hamster!

Michelle Knight (10)
Musbury Primary School, Axminster

Bullying

One day I walked down to the shop,
And I got some sweets to munch.
Some boys jumped out and said, *'Stop!'*
And gave me a dreadful punch.
They were tall and I was small,
They gave a shout and a clout.
I ran away and I said, *'Hooray,'* because they had gone.
I was scared because I was not prepared.

Susan Coalter (8)
Musbury Primary School, Axminster

Fast

I am so fast,
I am like a blast,
I am so quick,
I am like a flick,
I can jump so high,
I can't touch the sky.

James Satterley (10)
Musbury Primary School, Axminster

Snowman

Snowman is cold and round and soft.
The snowman slowly melts and disappears into the ground.
He is watching the children playing snow fights in the snow.
They are screaming like a crocodile.

Richard Ellis (7)
Musbury Primary School, Axminster

The Fast And The Furious

Agility shown in the face,
Aggressive but still with grace,
Down it comes,
Swooping down.
Will it hit the ground?

Fast it moves along the ground,
Oh no! There's a mound,
What will happen?
Who will see?
Will it tumble slowly?

It's coming close to the earth,
The ground is starting to stir,
Oh no! It's happening,
It has stopped,
The jaguar is dead!

Jack Irving (10)
Musbury Primary School, Axminster

Sadness

Hounds howling.
Horses trotting.
Hooves clattering.
Feet stamping.
Fear coming.
Red bushy tail shaking.
Black nose drying.
Paw aching.
Legs running.
Body bouncing.
Ears flapping.
Hats flying.
Barks raging.
Legs stopping.

Answer: Hunt.

Laura Parla (10)
Musbury Primary School, Axminster

Sunday Morning

I ask, 'What day is it Mum?'
She replies, 'Sunday.'
I say, 'What?'
She shouts, 'Sunday!'
'What?' I say
I get no reply
I ask, 'What day is it Dad?'
'Sunday son, go play bikes.'
'I can't, it's broke.'
'Go see Gran,' says Dad
'OK'
I go see Gran
She asks me,
'What day is it?'
I say, 'Oh Gran,
I don't know.'

Shannon Gibbs (11)
Nesting Primary School, Shetland

Why The Weather Is

'Why does the rain come from the sky?'
'It doesn't like coming from the ground.'
'Why is the sun so big?'
'The girl next door burped and it blew up like a balloon.'
'Why is the rainbow lots of colours?'
'It is seven colours of hair plaited together.'
'Why is fog not see-through?'
'It's the left over bubbles in the bath.'
'Why is hail so noisy on windows?'
'It wants inside to play with your toys.'

Rachel Smith (10)
Nesting Primary School, Shetland

I Wonder?

'Why's hail hard?'
'It's an angry giant throwing rocks.'
'Why's the fog so dense?'
'It's a god looking for a friend but he's shy.'
'Why's the sun bright?'
'It's a torch looking for its enemy.'
'Why's the rain damp?'
'It's just had a bath and it's dripping.'
'Why's the wind windy?'
'It's an athlete trying to break a world record for the fastest
person on Earth.'

Kirsty Bruce (11)
Nesting Primary School, Shetland

Why?

'Why is the snow cold?'
'The snow clouds forgot to put on the fire.'
'Why can't you see the wind?'
'The wind's secret identity would be found out if we could.'
'What makes rain?'
'It's a tap that someone left on.'
'Why is the snow white?'
'Someone forgot to send food colouring to the sky.'
'What is the sun?'
'It's a cooker in the sky cooking for all the animals on this land.'

Lauren Leask (10)
Nesting Primary School, Shetland

Why? Why? Why?

'Why is sleet slushy?'
'It's melted ice lollies slopping around in the bath.'
'Why is fog fluffy?'
'It's grey cotton buds floating in the sky.'
'Why does the wind whistle?'
'It's happy when it comes out to play.'
'Why does the sun sizzle?'
'It's cooking sausages for its tea.'
'Why is the snow slippery?'
'It likes to go sledging on slushy slopes.'

Karis Stevenson (10)
Nesting Primary School, Shetland

My Dog Jess

Jess my puppy is twelve weeks old
And she sits when she is told.

Her colour is black and tan
And she goes to work with my dad in his van.

She's not very big, actually she's quite small
And sometimes wees in our hall.

Her favourite toy is her squeaky lamb
And if I pinch it she may nip my hand.

When we walk her she likes to run in the woods
Puffing and panting, it does her good.

At night she likes to snuggle in my lap
And has a lovely long winter nap.

Jess our puppy is our best friend
And sometimes she drives me round the bend.

Alice Field (8)
Newport Community School, Barnstaple

My Dog Sam

My dog Sam
Is older but smaller than I am.
He's black and white with a long tail,
Which he wags a lot when he's happy.
He sleeps a lot when he is comfy,
When he is in a chair.
When Sam likes to take a nap
He usually does on Daddy's lap.
He had a stroke which made us sad,
Now he is better we are glad.
My dog Sam,
Is older but smaller than I am,
But I love him.

Emma Brice (8)
Newport Community School, Barnstaple

What's In The Zoo?

Zoo, zoo, what's in the zoo?
A monkey saying *o a o e*
A tiger that says *roar*
A mere cat going *eek*
A mouse that goes *squeak*

Zoo, zoo, what's in the zoo?
A bird flapping
A sea lion clapping
A zebra napping
And children chatting.
That's what's in the zoo.

China Blue Pascoe (8)
Newport Community School, Barnstaple

Chocolate

Easter is coming
The chocolate is running
Chocolate for breakfast
And chocolate for lunch
Chocolate for tea, oh and not forgetting brunch.

Chocolate chickens, chocolate bunnies,
Chocolate eggs in our chocolate tummies,
So much to choose from, so much to pick,
So much chocolate, I think I'll be sick!

Ruby Cumiskey (8)
Newport Community School, Barnstaple

A Butterfly

A butterfly up in the sky
How I like to watch you fly
Brightly coloured are your wings
You are such a beautiful thing
You fly around with such grace
You put a smile on my face.

Chloe Gratton (9)
Newport Community School, Barnstaple

Fairies

Fairies flutter through the air
With their purple dresses and golden hair.
They live under mushrooms and in trees
You normally hear about fairies in stories.
Fairies have magical powers
They could make it snow, rain or shine on flowers.
Most fairies wear a crown
And make you happy when you feel down.

Charlotte Rushton (9)
Newport Community School, Barnstaple

Seasons

S ee the baby lambs
P laying in the field
R iding on our bikes again
I n the park we can play
N ice to see the flowers coming
G reen leaves growing on the trees.

S miley faces everywhere, having fun on the beach
U mbrellas to shade you from the heat
M aking sandcastles one by one
M ust have an ice cream
E njoy playing in the sea
R unning from the waves - they might just catch me!

A ll the leaves fall off the trees
U ntil the trees are bare
T he rain is pattering down
U mbrellas we will need
M ay see a squirrel in our garden
N uts he will gather for the winter.

W rap up warm and cosy
I t's time to play in the snow
N eed a carrot for the snowman's nose
T wo eyes, a mouth and scarf
E xcited children everywhere
R udolph and Santa are on their way.

Jessica Lobb (8)
Newport Community School, Barnstaple

I Want A Hamster

If only Mum would let me have a hamster
I'd wash up every day
I'd clean my room and shine my shoes
And never get in the way.

Aiden Platt (10)
Newport Community School, Barnstaple

A Poem

I'm trying to write a poem
For this competition
It feels like a mission
I hope it gets into that book
If it does I'll have a look
I know my friend is going to do it
As she is a brilliant poet
I'm trying to do a poem for you
But I just don't know what to do!

Carrie-Ann Lane (10)
Newport Community School, Barnstaple

By The Seashore

On the seashore,
By the Caribbean Sea,
Curved brown coconuts
Swing in a tree.
Shells shimmer in the lovely
Horizon light,
People come in sheer delight.

Holly Colwill (10)
Newport Community School, Barnstaple

My Birthday

Strawberry ice cream on my nose,
Frosting ear to ear,
Feeding cake to the cat,
Party time is here.
Funny hats on all the pets,
Cola on the floor,
Although I'm turning eight today,
I'm acting like I'm four!

Tayler Horn (8)
Newport Community School, Barnstaple

Sweets

I love sweets,
They are treats!
Here's a few
I like to chew;
Lollies and Twix,
Pick 'n' mix
Sherbet dips,
Cherry lips,
Flake and Munchies,
Gum and Crunchies,
Chocolate drops,
Whistle pops.
But to follow,
Sugar you swallow
Teeth don't waste,
Use toothpaste!

Max Smith (10)
Newport Community School, Barnstaple

Milly And Max

Milly and Max, our mad dogs,
Milly is a mini terrier,
Max is a golden retriever.

They are soft,
They are sweet,
They are fun,
They are cuddly.

We walk them in the wet,
Running to the river,
Max jumps in,
Milly runs away.

Max has paws like a polar bear,
Milly has paws like a rat.

Ben Nethacott (9)
Newport Community School, Barnstaple

Guess What?

Heavy drinker,
Non thinker,
Fast speeder,
Modern leader,
Swift turner,
Road burner,
Gleaming racer,
Revving pacer,
Shining rager,
Style major.

Liam Undery (11)
Newport Community School, Barnstaple

Australian Sunset

The sun's rays trickling down the mountainside,
Shimmering on the crashing tide,
Falling quickly as the evening closes in,
As a dolphin glides you can see his fin.
Finally, as the sun disappears into the night
Gradually appearing, the glittering moonlight,
As the moon dawdles across the sky
I hear the sea let out a tired sigh.

Hannah Roy (10)
Newport Community School, Barnstaple

Aeroplane

Aeroplanes flying fast and high,
Trailing contrails in the sky,
Taking passengers to their destinations afar,
It's much faster than a car,
Wondering what they can see and do,
I bet they have fun, don't you?

Nathan Dover (9)
Newport Community School, Barnstaple

Lion

Tail sawyer,
Silent predator,
Meat eater,
Deer hunter,
Fast runner,
Lively roarer,
Bone cruncher,
Deep storer,
It's a swift lion.

Beckie Shortt (11)
Newport Community School, Barnstaple

Nibbles

Nibbles is my hamster.
He's round and soft and fluffy.
He has beady eyes and tiny feet
And a coat that's coloured honey.
He sleeps by day because it's light.
As soon as it's dark he likes to play all night.
He likes his tunnel slide and ball.
But he likes his wheel best of all.

Naomi Straughan (10)
Newport Community School, Barnstaple

The Mouse

There was a cat
He sat on a mat
His fur was covered in fleas
He licked his paws
And stuck out his claws
And that was the end of me.

Aaron Bennett (9)
Newport Community School, Barnstaple

Jackie Chan

J is for Jade, Jackie's young niece,
A is for amulet, a collectable piece
C is for Chui, sent by Daolon Wong to fight the clan,
K is for karate, a martial art from Japan.
I is for invisibility, snake talisman power,
E is for exciting, I read my magazine for hours.

C is for chi, a perfect state of mind,
H is for hero, the martial arts kind,
A is for action, it's adventure every day,
N is for ninja, trained the Japanese way.

Ryan Spencer (8)
Newport Community School, Barnstaple

My Christmas Cat

For Christmas this year I was given a cat,
Not a bat, or a hat, but a little fat cat.
He is only a kitten that fits in a mitten,
The colour of ginger, that chews on my finger,
I think he is nice, even if he chases mice,
That is my cat, not a bat or a hat.

Connor Wyatt (7)
Newport Community School, Barnstaple

Fairies

Do you know a fairy?
Fluttering in your room,
Waving her wand with magic,
Like a little pixie swiftly dancing around,
Going in your room at night so you,
Can see the glowing sight.
So you can see the wonderful sight of magical light!

Katie Ladley (9)
Newport Community School, Barnstaple

Treat With Care

Help people each day
As you go on your way.
When folks are blind
You should be kind.
When they can't hear
Talk loud and clear.
If they can't stand
Always lend a hand.
If he's wheelchair bound
You can push him around.
If she can't talk
Let her write with some chalk.
If her teeth are no good
You can mash up her food.
So remember be aware
Treat people with care.

Jade Harris (9)
Newport Community School, Barnstaple

Football

Eleven players in formation
Playing football for the duration.

The team looks smart in their new kit
The players must be very fit.

Lampard, Rooney, Owen, Scholes,
All have scored a lot of goals.

Dribbling, striking, passing, fouling
Rowdy crowds, a lot of howling.

The whistle blows - it's over now.

England has won - we ask but how?

Sam Pincombe (9)
Newport Community School, Barnstaple

Great White Shark

Film actor
Egg layer
World traveller
Evil grinner
Cunning hunter
Sneaky catcher
Body crusher
Deep dweller
Majestic mover
Nifty glider
Scare maker
Noisy thrasher
Slick swimmer
Carcass ripper
Blood smeller
Flesh eater.

Ross Kingsley (11)
Newport Community School, Barnstaple

Zoo Animal Poem

Elephants are fat and wide
They find it very hard to hide
Their trunks are very, very long
I wonder if they'd sing a song?

Parrots' colours are very bright
They make such a wonderful sight
They can squawk very, very loud
I wonder if they'd fly to a cloud?

A lion has a mighty roar
His fur is golden right to his paw
They are very, very clever cats
I wonder if they'd sit my SATs?

Myles Payne (9)
Newport Community School, Barnstaple

Thinking Horses

Welcome to 'Thinking Horses'
Here you can take your pony courses.

Hacking out in the sun
Can always lead to so much fun.

But hacking out in the rain
Can sometimes be a real pain!

I've got my reins in a muddle
I've steered my pony in a puddle!

Must get back for mucking out
Or instructor Sarah is bound to shout.

Stable chores never end
It sometimes drives me round the bend!

Soaping saddles and all the tack
It's not a place where you can slack.

In the yard is where we groom
To tidy up we use a broom.

My very last job of the day
Is to fill the hay nets full of hay.

I never want the day to end
As every pony is my friend.

Jessica Smith (9)
Newport Community School, Barnstaple

A Secret Box

Inside a box there are secrets never to be told.
The mysteries behind these secrets should never unfold.

The secrets are the deepest, the darkest and the worst,
And all of the secrets are haunted and cursed.

So never open the box, never touch the outside.
You don't want to see what's lurking inside!

Kathleen Acott (10)
Newport Community School, Barnstaple

Sweets

I love chocolate,
I love sweets,
I love sugar,
I love treats.

Healthy things are not my style,
Only sweet things are worthwhile.
Chocolate for breakfast - yum, yum yum,
Chocolate for lunch fills my tum.
Chocolate for dinner fills me up,
I don't eat vegetables they are yuk!

I love my sweeties lots and lots,
I love starbursts and jelly tots.

I'd like to get a swimming pool
And fill it all with sweets,
Then I would go diving
Into all the lovely treats.
I'd stay in there for hours and hours,
The best sight ever seen,
Then I'd have a sweetie shower,
It would be just like a dream.

Rhianna Draper (7)
Newport Community School, Barnstaple

My Little Brother

I have a little brother
He annoys me every day
Because when he's on the PlayStation
He never lets me play
He is OK sometimes
Although he's only eight
But when he eats with fingers
That's what I really hate
Then I look at his good points
And actually he is really great!

Laura Sherborne (11)
Newport Community School, Barnstaple

The Storm

As the Rain God spreads his tears over the land,
As the Wind Lord breathes his powerful breath,
As the Lightning God flicks the light on and off,
As the Thunder Lord stamps his feet in anger,
The people run aimlessly screaming in fear.

As the Water God unleashes his fury,
As the Hail Goddess shoots her icy bullets,
As the Snow Queen sprinkles her snowflakes of white,
As the Ice King spreads his ice sheets everywhere,
The land and people await their painful death.

Molly Fowler (11)
Newport Community School, Barnstaple

Animals

A is for an alligator swimming in a lake.
N is for a newt all slimy like a snake.
I is for Indian tiger, teeth as sharp as rakes.
M is for a monkey swinging in the trees.
A is for an aardvark running in the breeze.
L is for a leopard pouncing on anything that will pass.
S is for a snake slithering through the grass.

Tiana Muzard Clark (9)
Newport Community School, Barnstaple

My New School

I've started a new school,
It is really quite cool.
I'm early each day
Or Miss Kilham will have something to say.
We cross the road with the lollipop lady.
My sister cries, 'Oh what a baby.'

Kirby Thorne (7)
Newport Community School, Barnstaple

Cats

My favourite cats are fluffy and fat,
But I really, really like every cat.
Brown, grey, black or white
But please, please don't get in a fight.
They slink about in the dark, dark night
Giving every mouse they see a real fight.
They come back home in the morning to eat
They expect a really nice treat.

Jasmine Kent-Smith (8)
Newport Community School, Barnstaple

Fruit Loop

Plums are purple
Cherries come in twos
So much fruit
I just can't choose.

Apples are chewy
Oranges are fresh
Bananas are gooey
I like pears the best.

Amy Hooker (8)
Newport Community School, Barnstaple

Holy Festival Of Spring

The bonfire roars,
Flames redden my face,
Our coconut's roasting
At the base.
Dad's telling the story
Of Prahlad the Good,
While sparks fly up
From the crackling wood.

Jon Shaddick (8)
Newport Community School, Barnstaple

My Mum's Having A Baby

My mum's having a baby;
Pink clothes?
Blue clothes?
White clothes?
What to choose?

My mum's having a baby;
Small tummy,
Big tummy,
Enormous tummy,
How big will she get?

My mum's having a baby;
Kicking lots,
Wriggling lots,
Moving lots,
When will it sleep?

My mum's having a baby;
Stretchy tops,
Baggy trousers,
Tight coat,
Who does she look like?

My mum's having a baby;
Walking slowly,
Never running,
Stiff leg,
Where can she go?

My mum's having a baby;
Excited children,
Buying things,
Packing bags,
Why can't it be born now?

Bethany Clarke (7)
Newport Community School, Barnstaple

Rugby

It's Sunday, I get out of bed
With a yawn and a stretch.
It's rugby today, we'll soon be down on the pitch.

The opposition arrives
With a fairly strong side
But no match for our under ten side.

The whistle goes and right from the start
We trash and we bash, scoring tries as we go
That's how we play rugby in Barnstaple.

Harry Bentley (9)
Newport Community School, Barnstaple

Tsunami

On the beach the children played,
Laughing, shouting, having fun.
Sunbathers laying in the sun.
The disaster struck,
There was a great big wave.
Many people were very brave,
They lost homes and families too,
There is now so much for us to do,
They need lots of help from me and you.

Dale Leach (7)
Newport Community School, Barnstaple

Roast

R eally superb,
O utstanding meat,
A wesome potatoes,
S unday treat,
T errifying veg!

Samson Roberts (8)
Newport Community School, Barnstaple

I Met An Old Man

I met an old man
His name was Stan.

He was really tall
And good at pool.

His best friend was Paul
He went to school.

He had big toes
And a stuck-up nose.

He had a big house
And a very small mouse.

He had a big hat
And a little cat.

He had a big chair
And really weird hair.

Edie Dunkley (9)
Newport Community School, Barnstaple

My Dog

My dog is black and
Getting fat
But when she is good
We pat her back.

My dog is noisy
My dog is loud
When the doorbell
Rings she runs around.

When we are eating tea
She puts her head upon
My knee.

Charli Dellaway (10)
Newport Community School, Barnstaple

Dalmatians

D otty
A gile
L oving
M ellow
A ctive
T rustworthy
I ndependent
A lert
N eat
S ensible.

Rebecca Behnam (10)
Newport Community School, Barnstaple

Breeze

I swirl and curl
I wrestle and roll
I rumble and stumble
I freeze and sneeze

I blow and flow
I thunder and glide
I jump and jump

What am I?
A: The breeze.

Ysabel Thomas (9)
Newport Community School, Barnstaple

Back At School

Monday morning back at school.
I always go there as a rule.
Reading and writing through the day.
Learning lessons all the way.

George Critchard (9)
Newport Community School, Barnstaple

Magical Disneyland

One day I went to a magical place
Where all my dreams came true,
Mickey Mouse, Donald Duck,
Eeyore and Winnie the pooh.
My first stop was Frontier Land,
There was a haunted mansion
Which was very grand.
A runaway train and a freaky ghost,
That was the thing
That scared me the most.
In Discovery Land
I was whirled into space,
Which turned my stomach
And made my heart race.
The processions were wonderful
With all the princesses,
There were glittery lights
And long flowing dresses.
At the end of the day
Fireworks banged and they flashed,
Tinkerbell flew up to the castle
In a dash!

Myah Field (9)
Newport Community School, Barnstaple

Firework Night

F lying rockets zoom through the night sky.
I n the sky colours cascade.
R ainbow colours everywhere
E xcitement is in the air.
W onderful sparklers being waved about
O range bonfires on the ground.
R oaring sounds from loud bangs.
K ing-sized Catherine wheels spinning around.

Beth Westcott (9)
Newport Community School, Barnstaple

My Bedroom

The room that I go to
When I want to play
It's fun, fun, fun
And where I like to stay.

My friends will come to see me
Games to play is what we do
We all have the greatest fun
They all say, 'Well, thank you!'

At night it's time to sleep
Tucked up in bed warm and cosy
I read until lights out
It makes me feel quite dozy.

Morning is here, time to get up
Have a big yawn, out of bed I climb
School for me now work, work, work
Bye, bye my bedroom, see you at home time!

Georgia Rush (8)
Newport Community School, Barnstaple

Horses

Over the gate stood a mare and foal,
Their coats gleaming away in the sunlight
As if it were the sun looking at its reflection,
Their eyes glanced straight at me,
My heart pounded with glee,
I stepped closer,
They followed me,
I said, 'Shoo!'
And they fled,
With glee.

Charlotte Brend (10)
Newport Community School, Barnstaple

Football Player

If I played for Arsenal
I would be a centre-back
I would be so brilliant
The best player ever, in fact.

If I played for Arsenal
I could score all the time
I'd earn lots of money
And keep away from crime.

If I played for Arsenal
I would buy a sports car
And play in Madrid which is really,
Really far.

So when I grow up
I'm going to be a player
And if it falls through
I might just be the Mayor.

Callum Ford (7)
Newport Community School, Barnstaple

Family Silly Poem

I have a dog called Nash
And his hobbies are making mash.
I have another dog called Flow
She likes watching Teletubbies and her favourite's Po.
I have a mum called Sheila
And she likes drinking Tequila.
I have a dad called Mike
And he likes taking a hike.
I've got a brother called Ben
And he writes with a pen.
I've got a sister called Georgina
And she smells of Ribena.

Sam Collins (10)
Newport Community School, Barnstaple

Swimming

S wimming is my favourite sport
W inning is my aim
I train very hard six times a week
M y coaches can't complain
M any medals I have won
I would love to swim for Great Britain one day
N ever give up, got to win
G old is the only way.

Justin Southam (10)
Newport Community School, Barnstaple

Goalkeeping

I dive to the left, then to the right
To keep this goal empty I have to put up a fight
Muddy boots and muddy gloves this is the sport all boys love
The pressure mounts as the striker comes near
But I will not show any fear
I stand my ground as he takes aim . . .
It hits the crossbar.
Oh what a shame!

Charles Rogers (10)
Newport Community School, Barnstaple

Football

I played with my football
Against a big wall
I was having great fun
Till Mum gave me a call
Up went the red card
Down went the ball
She dragged me home
By my big earhole.

Harry Thomas (8)
Newport Community School, Barnstaple

Unicorns

Unicorns are timid
They hide away at sounds of human footsteps
They prance and dance all day
While nibbling on grass and leaves

Unicorns live in enchanted places
Where creatures talk
Where people cannot set foot
Where they may roam free

Unicorns are beautiful
With long silver manes
With glittery golden hooves
And a horn that sparkles in the sun.

Gemma Wells (9)
Newport Community School, Barnstaple

Starfish

Starfish, starfish
Where would you be?
In the ocean, in the sea?
Starfish, starfish
Orange and bright,
Swimming in the water
Shimmering in the light.
Starfish, starfish,
Caught in a net,
Kept as an ornament
Though still wet.
Starfish, starfish,
Now so dry,
But there always comes
A time to die.

Isabelle Braidwood (10)
Newport Community School, Barnstaple

Basketball

B ouncing the ball up and down the court.
A lways trying to speed up the game.
S hooting the ball to score a three pointer.
K eeping the ball amongst your team mates.
E motions go high when the teams score again.
T ense moment near the end of the game.
B alls are bouncing into the crowd.
A ction everywhere, up and down the court.
L ong passes, if there's no one in the way.
L akers are the best team by far.

Shane Prater (10)
Newport Community School, Barnstaple

My Pet

Run, stop, look,
Apple, grass and hay nibbler,
Burrowing down,
Bouncing high,
Inquisitive and nosy,
Thump, thump, bang, bang,
Snuggles down to sleep,
What is my pet?

Patrick French (8)
Newport Community School, Barnstaple

Winter

W indy winter
I cy rooftops
N orth cold
T hick snow
E xciting snowflakes
R ainy days.

Jacob McCowen-Smith (8)
Newport Community School, Barnstaple

My Cat Is A Bother

My cat is a bother
So says my mother
We have a name for him
But he's really quite dim
When we call 'Mysti'
He ignores us
But when it's food time
He adores us
He's fluffy, ginger and white
But he's not so light
He often brings in presents
And leaves them on the floor
But Mum screams and shouts
And throws him out the cat flap in the door.

Chandler Tregaskes (8)
Newport Community School, Barnstaple

Aston Villa

A very good football team
S orensen is the goalkeeper
T enth in the league
O lef Melberg is a good tackler
N obby Solano is a great midfielder

V assell is an excellent forward
I would like to play for them when I'm older
L ove going to watch them at Villa Park
L uke Moore tackles hard
A ngel is my favourite player.

Lewis Hall (8)
Newport Community School, Barnstaple

Walk In The Dark

W hen I took a walk in the dark.
A ll the cars zoomed by.
L ights were shining on the ground.
K aleidoscope colours.

I t was a dark and rainy night.
N ot a single thing was out.

T he birds were all in their nests.
H edgehogs were hunting for slugs.
E verything seemed to be listening.

D on't be afraid of the dark.
A ll the same things are there in the day.
R ight now I am snuggled up by the fire.
K nowing it is dark outside!

Charlotte Wotton (9)
Newport Community School, Barnstaple

My Island

My island
Has the blue sea
Lapping onto
The golden sand
There is a coconut tree
And a cheeky monkey passes a coconut to me
There is a little beach hut
I sit in there with my tropical drink
I come to my island
When I am asleep
I spend hours on my island
I love it.

Alice Leaman (8)
Newport Community School, Barnstaple

Houses

Houses, here,
Houses there,
Houses in the rain.

Houses small,
Houses tall
Houses everywhere.

Houses blue
As the sky
Houses green
Really clean.

Houses yellow,
Houses orange.
Houses bright
Full of light.

Danielle Anderson (8)
Paible School, Loch Maddy

My Pet Dog

When I come
Home from school
I see my dog
She wags her tail.

Wag, wag, wag
She jumps on me.
Jump, jump, jump
All over me.

She has a
Black and white tail.
I love her so much
I want to squeeze her head.

Margaret MacDougall (9)
Paible School, Loch Maddy

Guns

'Gun, gun
Where have you been?'
'I've been shooting
Out on the hill.'

'Gun, gun
What did you get?'
'I got a duck
A duck to pluck.

I also got
Some big, fat geese.
But who came along?
The obese police!'

Ruairidh MacDonald (9)
Paible School, Loch Maddy

I Hate This Day

I hate this day
You're a stinky sister
And so is my brother
Even Mum and Dad are nicer
Than you are.

Neil MacLean (7)
Paible School, Loch Maddy

Faces

Faces here
Faces there
Faces fighting
Everywhere
All you can see
Are faces
You see them everywhere.

Katie Hocine (9)
Paible School, Loch Maddy

When I Am Old

When I am old
I shall be stacked with gold
And my house
Shall be free from mould.

I shall live in New York
With my pet pork.
I shall call him Lenz
And he shall live with my hens.

I shall have a motorbike
To take me to the school
To pay the teachers
To go on strike.

I shall have six dogs
And they won't be hogs.
I'll take them for walks
In amongst the logs.

When I die
I shall lose my gold
And my house shall be
Full of mould.

Lara Bulmer (9)
Paible School, Loch Maddy

Stinky Parents And Sis

Mum is as fat as a plum
Dad is very bad
Sis eats a moth
Covered in a cloth.

My sis ate a magic muffin
And she is a big fat puffin.
My mum still has chicken pox
And she's in love with Tony Hawkes.

Fazel Froughi (7)
Paible School, Loch Maddy

Giants

Giants here
Giants there
Giants hunting bears.

Giants far
Giants near
Giants hunting deer.

Giants here
Giants there
Giants everywhere.

John A MacDonald (9)
Paible School, Loch Maddy

Snow Day

When I go out for a fight
The snow is very white.
I play outside
I throw a snowball at my sister.
I rolled up a snowball,
It turned into a snowman
And then it said, 'Hello!'

Andrew MacSween (7)
Paible School, Loch Maddy

My Fat Cat

On Monday my mum gave me a cat.
But when it came in I realised it was fat.

I agreed with my mum that I would keep her
Because she was a whole lot cheaper.

The cat goes to bed at nine and actually wakes up on time.
It loves to play with the dog who enjoys to sleep on a log.

Hannah Hocine (7)
Paible School, Loch Maddy

My Dog

She runs about the house and jumps on me
And chases cats up a tree.
Her name is Lucky
And she is always mucky.

She hates cats
And sleeps on two mats.
She loves to play
And never rests all day.

She always barks
And is scared of the dark.
She is brown and white
And likes to fight.

She chews on my shoes all the time
And likes to eat lime.
She has a friend called Chloe
And likes it when it is snowy.

Catriona Fyfe (9)
Paible School, Loch Maddy

Books

Yellow books
Green books
Books everywhere
Books in my wardrobe
And books in my lair.

Math books
Round books
Textbooks
Everywhere
Oh no!
Too many books
Are in my lair!

Joshua Crow (9)
Paible School, Loch Maddy

The Old Car

There is a car
That can drive very far
It is very old
And full of mould
It is full of rust
And a lot of dust
It has three wheels
And it's made from steel
A tyre has been burst by a fork
And it doesn't really work.

Fraser MacDonald (9)
Paible School, Loch Maddy

Wishes

I wish I was a monster
I wish I was a fairy
I wish I was a millionaire
I wish I could do better in school
I wish I could touch the sky
I wish I was an alien
I wish I was with my family and friends.
I wish . . .

Kemi Shasanya (8)
Redwood Junior School, Derby

Once I Had A Kitten

Once I had a kitten,
It chewed on my favourite mitten.
Kittens grow into cats,
Cats always eat rats,
But they hate bats.

Do you like cats?

Shakira Sangha (7)
Redwood Junior School, Derby

What Is Friendship?

'What is friendship?'
'Friendship is like a sunny day.'

'When does it mostly happen?'
'Mostly in May.'

'Who are your friends?'
'Kamara and Holly.'

'How did you meet them?'
'I met them in school
And showed them my dolly.'

'What did you show them?'
'I showed them my money.'

'What did you give them to eat?'
'I gave them some honey.'

Melissa Dawson (7)
Redwood Junior School, Derby

Giraffe

A giraffe has long legs
But when he is hungry
He eats branches.

Giraffes sound like they are not real,
They sometimes sound like seals.

A tall giraffe can play with a ball,
A small giraffe bumps into walls.

A giraffe has a sticky tongue,
But he is not really very strong.

Samantha Smedley (11)
Redwood Junior School, Derby

My Strange Neighbourhood

My neighbourhood is the
Strangest place on Earth:

There's cats chasing
Dogs and frogs,
Trees and birds and
Dogs eating cat food,
Flies eating frogs,
Dogs climbing trees,
And mice eating cats.

Casey Weir (7)
Redwood Junior School, Derby

Once I Had A Puppy

Then it chewed on my shoe.
Then he said, 'Moo!'
Then he said, 'I am Sue.'
Then he said, 'I am coming too.'
Then he said, 'I am going to the loo.'
Then he said, 'I am poor!'

Leeanda Alderton (7)
Redwood Junior School, Derby

Jess

Jess is white with a pink nose,
With a cute look on her face,
She prowls about at night looking for food,
She purrs the cutest purr I have ever heard.
Jess has a toy mouse that jingles when she gets it.
Once I saw her on the windowsill,
I think Jess is the best cat in the world.

Luke Beatson (8)
Ridgeway Primary School, Ridgeway

Winter Playtime

A teacher standing by the wall.
The children playing happily.
Blue sky with big white clouds in.
A big shed on the other side of the playground.
A peace garden next to the shed.
A football pitch in the middle.
The wind going *whoosh, whoosh* in the trees.
The children shouting and screaming.
The bell going at the end of play.

Harriet Lockett (7)
Ridgeway Primary School, Ridgeway

My Family

My dad is bad,
My mum is sad,
But worst of all my brother is mad.

My uncle is crazy,
My grandad is lazy,
But best of all my nan grew a daisy.

Brooke Woolley (8)
Ridgeway Primary School, Ridgeway

The Weirdest Sister!

My sister is weird, very weird indeed!
She can beat you at cheating and falling down.
My mum thinks she's a nutter and so do I.
She is so weird that I could die.
She can beat you at burping and sleeping on a horse.
She laughs like a monkey and walks like a horse.
She is weird of course.

India Nelson (8)
Ridgeway Primary School, Ridgeway

My Brother

My brother has a cute look,
He screams and squeals,
He rolls and rolls to the other side,
He says, 'Ga, ga, goo, ga, ba, da'
He eats baby food,
He sleeps in his cot,
He sometimes goes in the bath with me,
My brother is the cutest baby in the universe.

Maisie Jameson (7)
Ridgeway Primary School, Ridgeway

Billy The Baby

Babies are fun,
Babies can't run,
You hear 'Dada' all the time,
They like a good rhyme,
When they go to sleep,
You can have a peep,
They can't write,
They can't drink Sprite.

Joshua Collins (7)
Ridgeway Primary School, Ridgeway

Bonny

Bonny is big,
Bonny is tall,
It does not matter at all,
Bonny is creamy and like the sunset,
Jumps like a rocket setting off,
Runs like a cheetah,
Her coat breezes in the wind like a tree,
When you touch her hair, it's all soft like a bed.

Louis Barrie (7)
Ridgeway Primary School, Ridgeway

The Flower Poem

Violets are blue,
Roses are red.
The smell of flowers,
Are always in your head.
You can never stop smelling them,
Wherever you go.
Flowers smell like raspberry,
And all sorts too.
You want to pick them,
But that is cruel.
They are so beautiful,
And colourful too.
You've got to like flowers,
Tell me the truth.
Big, medium and small,
All sorts of sizes.
You get the feeling of happiness,
Inside your heart.
Flowers are bright,
And also light.
The bees are gathering honey,
And are also wanting food.
There are lots of petals,
And a middle too.

Elise Davidson (7)
Ridgeway Primary School, Ridgeway

Winter Playground

I walk outside on a windy day,
I feel cold on my face,
A ball flying across my face,
Children with scarves on,
Cars racing past me,
Kites flying high in the sky.

Joseph Shires (7)
Ridgeway Primary School, Ridgeway

My Best Friend

My best friend has got straight hair,
My best friend is not scared of a bear,
My best friend likes to swim by the beach,
My best friend would like a peach,
My best friend likes to read a book,
My best friend is not allowed to cook,
My best friend goes to the fair,
My best friend has got brown hair,
My best friend makes me giggle,
My best friend's bum wiggles,
My best friend goes to Spain,
My best friend dances in the rain,
My best friend likes her drink lemony,
My best friend is called Emily,
My best friend likes to play, I Spy,
My best friend says, 'Bye, bye!'

Holly Dickinson (8)
Ridgeway Primary School, Ridgeway

Winter Playground

When I walk outside, with a slight breeze,
I can't get warm, *brrr!*
When I get in the playground I freeze,
Trees sway in the breeze.
The ground is white,
The grass is green,
The sky's blue,
The colourful flowers swing side to side.
People scream in the playground,
The wind *whooshes,*
The cars go *vrrrm!*
The litter will fly in the sky.

Luke Longmuir (8)
Ridgeway Primary School, Ridgeway

The Alphabet

A is for Annie who likes toast
B is for Ben who bumped in a post
C is for Charlotte who likes eating
D is for Darren who likes cheating
E is for Emily who loves planes
F is for Frank who likes ants
G is for Gail who has a small house
H is for Harriet who has a pet mouse
I is for India who loves wearing hats
J is for Jack who has a pet cat.

Annie Wood (7)
Ridgeway Primary School, Ridgeway

A Winter Playtime

The sting on your face as you step outside,
The sun is cold.
Children laughing and talking and playing.
The deep wintry sky above, with a smile upon his face,
The lost mixture of colours on the floor like standing on a rainbow.
Yet nothing seems to be different each and every day.

Matthew Rowland (7)
Ridgeway Primary School, Ridgeway

My Cat Jazy

Jazy in my garden chasing mice and rats
Jazy purring and scratching the door,
When she wants to come in.
Jazy is black, white and orange
Jazy is nice when she is asleep.

Thomas Radcliffe (8)
Ridgeway Primary School, Ridgeway

Those Who Lurk Around In The Dark

When it's dark those who lurk around
When you're in bed, they make very strange sounds.
They make snorting and panting
And groaning and moaning
And the floorboards creak in your house!
Maybe it's coming up the stairs,
Maybe it's got lots of hairs,
You slip under your cover
Then you scream for your mother.

When it's dark those who lurk around
When you go and look they can never be found.
They hiss and they snarl as they creep through the night
Your heart is thumping as you reach for the light.
You see your curtains moving and it gives you a fright,
And then something jumps out and says . . .
'Boo!'

Sam Vessey (10)
Ridgeway Primary School, Ridgeway

My Family Poetry

I am the youngest in the family all day and night
Soon I'll be the second youngest
Dad is crazy, crazy about football, he never stops
Hannah never stops talking about fashion
Thomas goes on his PS2
Grandad Jones asks so many questions
Grandad Blackburn is as deaf as a post
Nan-nan Blackburn lets me sleep
Grandma Jones is poorly, but nice
Coby is the one I know and so bright.

Lauren Jones (7)
Ridgeway Primary School, Ridgeway

Colours

White is as white as thick snow
Cream is like the colour of champagne
Yellow is as bright as the sunshine
Orange is as beautiful as the sunset
Pink is as pink as a flamingo
Red is like a glowing apple
Lilac is just like a flower petal
Blue is like the light sky
Green is like the shining grass
Grey is as dull, as dawn in the gloomy night
Brown is as brown, as a big sausage
Black is as black forever.

Ava Jenkinson (8)
Ridgeway Primary School, Ridgeway

Winter Playground

It's very sunny
I can feel the breeze over my hand
People screaming in the wind
The gravel is black
The sun is going down
Time to go in
The play is nearly over
We arc doing our lessons now

Jacob Duffy (7)
Ridgeway Primary School, Ridgeway

Whales

You see blue whales whisking by,
They squirt shiny blue water.
Hear their lovely singing echoes in the sea.
Smell the fishy smell of barnacles.

Charles Sidney (8)
Ridgeway Primary School, Ridgeway

Summer Park

Sunshine beams on the river.
Colourful flowers everywhere.
Families having picnics with yummy food.
People sunbathing,
People rowing on the river.
My favourite bit is the yummy ice cream.
I love the park when the sun is shining.

Emily Rhodes (8)
Ridgeway Primary School, Ridgeway

The Spell For A Good Team

Get a good pitch
Make sure there's no ditch
Bake a good team
Let flow the steam
Pour some teamwork in the pot
Stir it round for the lot
Bake it, burn it, grill it well
Run carefully so your apple doesn't swell
Add a manager, stir him up
One that wants to win the cup
Get some subs on the bench
It doesn't matter if they speak French
Stir the striker to shoot in the net
It'll make the supporters bet
Bake it, burn it, grill it well
Run carefully so your ankle doesn't swell
Burn the goalie gloves, stir them in
Be polite or they'll make a din
Add in the players' boots
Or they'll start to loot
Make flags for the corners
Or the ref will be a yawner
Bake it, burn it, grill it well
Run carefully so your ankle doesn't swell.

Luke Moody (11)
St John's CE Primary School, Worksop

My Pet

My pet is a dog,
He likes to play on every log.
He chases cats up the street
Because he thinks he will get a treat.

My pet is a cat,
He sits on the red mat.
He always loves his lunch
Because he makes a big munch.

My pet is a fish,
She always tries to get on a dish.
She flips her tail in the water,
She acts like she is our daughter.

My pet is a rabbit,
She always gets into a habit.
She loves to have lots of carrots,
She always chases parrots.

Gemma Boyd (8)
St John's CE Primary School, Worksop

The Charge Of The Fly Brigade

Half an inch, half an inch,
Half an inch onwards,
Into cat valley,
As they ride forward.

'Forward fly brigade,
Get ready to rumble!'
They pushed over the cat,
What a big tumble.

Backwards to the right of them,
Backwards to the left of them,
Backwards to the back of them,
'Bite his bum!' he said.

Katie D'Avila (9)
St John's CE Primary School, Worksop

Tsunami Disaster

Let's now stop what we're doing
And say a few words,
To the towns and the villages with no singing birds,
To the people destroyed, trying to get a tan,
They had nothing to do, they just ran and ran.
Many days this went on for, loved ones dead,
No place to remember, but mass graves instead,
Tears falling like trickles of rain,
Those tears represent loved ones' pain.
The lands like Asia and many more,
Cannot look into an open door,
All that can be done is pray and pray,
Hoping people like you, give something today.
So think right now, give a thought,
To people dying, families distraught.

Hannah Steeper (11)
St John's CE Primary School, Worksop

The Galloping Mare

The graceful mare galloped across the land,
Mane and tail gleaming in the bright light,
Her massive hooves, hooves hitting the golden sand,
To see her trotting was a splendid sight,
Her pretty body, as white as the moon,
Her beautiful eyes, twinkled like stars,
It was getting dark, night would fall soon,
No doubt she was the prettiest by far,
She tossed her head back and gave a loud neigh,
She stopped to take a drink from the river,
Then she felt hungry, she nibbled on hay,
As it got colder she began to shiver,
In the morning, when the cockerel crows,
She will be off again, up hills, down roads.

Ellie Trewick (10)
St John's CE Primary School, Worksop

The Playground

Skip, skip
Hop, hop
Run around the hopscotch
Jump, jump
Hop, hop
Run around the playground
Run, run
Hop, hop
Run around the lollipop lady
Creep, creep
Hop, hop
Run around the teacher
Walk, walk
Hop, hop
Run around the little tree
Jog, jog
Hop, hop
Run around the big log
Tiptoe, tiptoe
Hop, hop
Run around the whole school.

Laura Toon (8)
St John's CE Primary School, Worksop

Cats

Cats are big, cats are small,
Kittens are little, grown cats are tall,
If they see a squeaky mouse,
Cats will chase it around the house.
Cats like to play with balls of wool,
They like to eat until they're full.
They like to nap upon your lap.
They like their very own cat flap.
Cats are free and like to roam,
When they're hungry, they always come home.

Hannah Dixon (10)
St John's CE Primary School, Worksop

My Best Friend

My best friend
Is Natasha
She's cool and she's fun
And she likes to run
She's funny
Her favourite animals are
Dolphins, elephants
Cats, dogs, kittens and puppies
Her favourite food is
Tuna bake and ice cream
That's my best friend
And Cathryn is the same
But she's
Weird and silly
And her favourite animals are
Squirrels and bunnies
And her favourite food is
Flapjack and pasta
And she's a best friend too
But me, Cathryn and Natasha
Will always be best friends
And that's true.

Jessica Davies (8)
St John's CE Primary School, Worksop

Cats

Cats, cats are such lovely things,
They hate bees because they give them bad stings.
When they go to sleep, they curl up in balls,
When they want their food, they begin to call.
When they find mice, they pounce
And when they like something, they start to purr,
Cats are such lovely things.

Georgia Field (10)
St John's CE Primary School, Worksop

Oh Yes, Oh No!

Oh yes, oh yes,
My baby cousin is coming,
Oh yes, oh yes,
I get to feed him,
Oh no, oh no,
He spits it back at me

Oh yes, oh yes,
I get to play with him
Oh yes, oh yes
He's under the play gym
Oh no, oh no
He's pulling my hair

Oh no!

Elicia Hibbard (9)
St John's CE Primary School, Worksop

My Cats

My cats sleep on the floor
And try to open the cat food door.
My cats like to play,
In fact they like to play all day.
My cats like to fight,
Even if it takes all night.
My cats' names are Kes and Bruno.

Alex Winter (9)
St John's CE Primary School, Worksop

My Grandma

My grandma is good
My grandma is the nicest grandma in the world
And she is that forever
And it should stay like that.

Liam Curley (8)
St John's CE Primary School, Worksop

My Grandad

My grandad is very funny
He wipes his custard on his top
He acts like a clown
Runs like a dog
And likes to jump over the playground log
My grandad is very funny
He wipes his gravy on his trousers
He acts like a baby
Jumps like a bunny
And likes to suck on my sister's dummy

My grandad is very funny
He wipes his tomato ketchup on his shoes
He acts like a girl
Wears lots of pearls
And wears a wig that has curls
My grandad is very funny
He wipes his cream on his coat
He acts like a monkey
Hangs from trees
And he always eats the leaves

My grandad is very funny
He wipes his greasy fingers on his jacket
He acts like a frog
He likes to jump in piles of leaves
And likes to snap branches off trees
My grandad is very funny
He wipes his nose on . . .
He's going to wipe his nose on me
Help! Help! Help!

Jade Plumridge (9)
St John's CE Primary School, Worksop

My Best Friend

My best friend
Her name is Cathryn
She's cool
She's fun and she loves a big bun
Her favourite food is
Pasta, sticky rice, chillies
Curry, fish, octopus, crab
Chicken, strawberries, cheesecake
Yoghurt, ice cream, cakes
Chocolate, jelly and fruit salad
Her favourite animals are
Hamsters, rabbits, gerbils and squirrels
And that's my best friend.

Natasha Hall (9)
St John's CE Primary School, Worksop

Police

Police are quick
Police are strict
And police always are arresting
They work all day
Looking after people
And never stop chasing
Criminals on the street
At the station screaming and banging
On the doors
So they lock them.

Connor Allison (9)
St John's CE Primary School, Worksop

A Simile Poem

As green as a cucumber on a plate,
As orange as a new painted gate.
As yellow as little grains of sand,
As gold as a ring on someone's hand.
As blue as a new ink pen,
As blond as hair on some men.
As brown as a big silly monkey,
As grey as an old dopey donkey.

Amy Jackson (10)
St John's CE Primary School, Worksop

I Love Skipping

Skipping, skipping, I love skipping,
Keep on going, 120, 121,
I want to stop, but I can't,
Puff, puff, keep on going,
Puff, puff, keep on going,
I want to stop,
Now I'm going to stop . . . Now I'm . . .
Going home to rest, *zzzzz.*

Millie Gascoyne (8)
St John's CE Primary School, Worksop

My Sister, Sophie

My sister, Sophie is good in every way
But sometimes she gets on my nerves
But me and my sister are great in every way
Sometimes we fight and sometimes we don't
But just together, we are great in every way
And always she wants to play with me.

Holly Leinster (9)
St John's CE Primary School, Worksop

At The Park

Run through the gate
Slide down the slide
Race your mate
Have a bike ride

Swing on the swings
Splash in the pool
Hear the girls sing
Mr Cool

Have a game of tig
Play a little footy
Have a little dig
Eat a chocolate cookie

Go and climb the stairs
That look like a comb
Now it's time
To go home.

Sophie Fletcher (11)
St John's CE Primary School, Worksop

Molly

Molly can be great!
Molly can be fun!
Molly can be rotten!
Molly can be mean!
I love Molly no matter,
I love Molly because
She's the best
Sister
You
Would
Ever
Want.

Poppy Goodall (8)
St John's CE Primary School, Worksop

What Is Colour?

What is blue?
Blue is the sky, blue is the sea, so don't ask me.
Blue is a book, blue is paint, so don't tell the saints.

What is red?
Red is an apple, red is a poppy, so don't go hoppy.
Red is blood, red is fire, so don't go higher.

What is green?
Green is grass, green is a sweet, so don't go tweet.
Green is a pen, green is some leaves, so don't cut the trees.

What is pink?
Pink is a pig, pink is a pencil, so don't make a stencil.
Pink is my skin, pink is a rose, so don't pose.

What is purple?
Purple is a felt tip, purple is a tray, so don't get some hay.
Purple is my jumper, purple is a sign, so don't go fine.

What is a rainbow?

Bryony Proctor (8)
St John's CE Primary School, Worksop

Why Me?

'Why me, Mum? I always wash up.'
'Why me, Dad? I always wait for the loo.'
'Why me, Sister? I always tidy up.'
'Why me, Ben? I'm always lost.'
'Why me, Teacher? I always get extra homework.'
'Why me?'

'Why me, Gran? I always collect the eggs.'
'Why me, Grandad? I always feed the pigs.'
'Why me, Aunty? I always look after Baby Bob.'
'Why me?'
'Why you, Heather?' said Mum
'You are always in front of the TV!'

Heather Fothersgill (8)
St John's CE Primary School, Worksop

Playground Roots

Children playing
Parents moaning
Children swinging
Parents groaning

Children eating
Parents arguing
Children fighting
Parents happy

Horses jumping
Ducks swimming
Horses riding
Ducks eating

Horses trotting
Ducks flying
Horses hurdling
Ducks showing off.

Charlie Young (11)
St John's CE Primary School, Worksop

Something Strange

There's something strange in the hall
But I can hear them having a ball
They're thumping, bashing, crashing
All of the lightning is flashing

Crash, bang, clip, clang.

I wonder what they're doing?
Something strange is cooing
Hear them playing around
They are making a loud sound.

Crash, bang, clip, clang.

Katie Ashmore (10)
St John's CE Primary School, Worksop

Snowy Weather

Snowballs are wet
Snowballs are cold
You throw them at people if they like them
You have a fight in the playground
And make them large and small

Make snowmen, make snowballs
Practise building snowmen in the grass

It's fast and wet
You get it on your head
Make sure you wrap up
So you don't get cold
And it settles eventually, it settles

Make snowmen, make snowballs
Practise building snowmen on the grass

You can do sledging on the snowy ground
When doing it, it's very fast
You turn left and right
And sometimes you do sledging on the grass
You dig your shoes in the snow to stop.

Matthew Beck (11)
St John's CE Primary School, Worksop

Football Teams

Football players on the pitch
Away supporters in a ditch
All cheering for their team
While eating delicious ice cream

Manager shouting from the bench
While dancing with someone French
People chatting, clitter-clack
While having their name put on a plaque
Man U, Sheffield Wednesday, all the teams
While their kit shines and gleams.

Jack Barnes (11)
St John's CE Primary School, Worksop

Oh No!

Oh yes, oh yes, the waiter's coming
Oh yes, oh yes, with a glass of Coke
Oh yes, oh yes, he's heading to me
Oh no, oh no, he's spilt it all over my lap

Oh yes, oh yes, the waiter's coming
Oh yes, oh yes, with a slice of pizza
Oh yes, oh yes, he's heading to me
Oh no, oh no, he's dropped it down my front

Oh yes, oh yes, the waiter's coming
Oh yes, oh yes, with a plate of chips
Oh yes, oh yes, he's heading to me
Oh no, oh no, it's landed on my mum's knee

Oh yes, oh yes, the waiter's coming
Oh yes, oh yes, with a bowl of ice cream
Oh yes, oh yes, he's heading to me
Oh no, oh no, he's dropped it on my head

Oh no, oh no, the waiter's coming
Oh no, oh no, with something
Oh no, oh no, he's heading to me
Oh no, oh no, it's only the bill, lucky it says nil.

Emily Davies (8)
St John's CE Primary School, Worksop

Teachers

Teachers can be bossy and mean,
They say your classmates are your team,
They can shout at you when you've done nothing wrong,
So when they turn around, stick out your tongue,
If a teacher read this, they'd go completely mad
And if you've done something wrong, they'll say you're really bad,
But my teacher isn't like that at all, she's ace
And never has a long face!

Ellie Fox (10)
St John's CE Primary School, Worksop

Animal ABC

A nts creeping,
B ears growling,
C aterpillars crawling,
D ogs barking,
E lephants trumpeting,
F rogs croaking,
G iraffes crunching,
H ares running,
I guanas sleeping,
J ackals hunting,
K angaroos jumping,
L eopards sprinting,
M onkeys hanging,
N ewts swimming
O rang-utans itching,
P olar bears sniffing,
Q ueen bees buzzing,
R ats scampering,
S nakes hissing,
T igers killing,
U nicorns head-butting,
V oles hiding,
W alrus flapping,
X tremely deadly vipers snatching,
Y aks yapping,
Z ebras stripy.

Molly Goodall (11)
St John's CE Primary School, Worksop

Dinner Time

Let's go outside to play right now,
Why not be polite and take a bow.
Our colour goes zoom round the corner,
Take off your shoes, it's like a sauna.
Line up it will take forever,
Talk to your friend, she is called Heather.
Just grab your tray, knife and fork,
With this beautiful food you will not bauk.
Pick your food, whichever you like,
There could be a fish just like a pike.
Get your dessert with a bit of custard,
But be careful, don't get mixed up with mustard.
Grab a cup with a lot of juice,
They might just give you a chocolate mousse.
Their food is so, so nice,
Join together, sing for joy like mice.
Take your tray to the table,
With your dinner, watch some cable.
Get your dinner, gulp it down,
You're being entertained by Krusty the clown.
When you've finished, empty your tray,
Just be kind and don't forget to pray.
Get your shoes, go back outside,
There's a bit of mud, don't you slide.
The whistle goes, it's end of play,
You might go inside and do art with clay.
It's boring for people in class,
Just wait till tomorrow, there will be another clash.

Ellice Pettinger (11)
St John's CE Primary School, Worksop

The Children's Image Of Fun

Enter the world of laughter
Hear the voices to be heard
See the trees leaning to me
The parents don't say a word

Sunflowers tall
Bluebells ring
School bell chimes
A ring-a-ding-ding

A park makes games fun
Puts smiles on every face
Tigging, swimming, diving and running
You just go at your own pace

Roses sprouting
Daisies white
Buttercups yellow
Making your chin bright

The park is fun for everyone
You can play all day long
Come to the park today
It is only a walk away.

Sophie Cashmore (11)
St John's CE Primary School, Worksop

What Is Green?

The grass is green and the plants are too,
The trees' leaves are green and crayons are too,
A jacket is green and sweets are too,
Broccoli is green and paper is too,
A hat is green but make sure your hair is not green!

Ashley Bond (7)
St John's CE Primary School, Worksop

Weather

I like the snow when it blows in the wind.
I like spring when the blossoms are growing.
The birds are singing in the trees.
Summer is here, spring has gone.
Summer is hot, the sun is red.
The last season, autumn, red, orange, gold and green.
What beautiful colours ever seen.
Weather is a wonderful thing.

Roxanna Hood (8)
St John's CE Primary School, Worksop

Snowball

S nowballs are round
N ow it's flat
O opsy, I didn't do it!
W ow! I put it back together again
B ang, right on the garden shed
A rgh, ouch, that hurt
L ong shot there friend
L ong shot away to you.

Jack Dronfield (8)
St John's CE Primary School, Worksop

Sports

In sports you play rugby and football,
In football you score a goal.
In rugby you score a try and drop-goal.
In cricket you hit a six and four.
In hockey you try and score.
In basketball you get a slam-dunk
And that's the way to score and win.

Kieran Blood (11)
St John's CE Primary School, Worksop

Food

I only like good food
But sometimes I'm not in a good mood
I always have to have a pudding after my lunch
It makes a nice big crunch
For my breakfast I have cereal every day
Because I think I'm in a hotel bay
I always eat my breakfast to make me strong
Because I want to be long
Then I want to have some chips
Because they have them on the ships
I don't like nets on fish
Only when it's in the dish
I always eat Christmas dinners
I think sausages are the winners.

Thomas Gladwin (8)
St John's CE Primary School, Worksop

The White Witch

The white witch is very sly
She thinks she can make Aslan die
The white witch has a pale white face
She made Narnia a cold and snowy place
The white witch is so evil and cruel
That she thinks she can rule

The white witch turns the rivers into ice
She never wants to be kind or nice
She can never keep a deal
She even hates the cutest seals
Her face is as white as snow
She's evil and cruel from head to toe.

Beth Rowett (10)
St John's CE Primary School, Worksop

Playing In The Snow

Playing in the snow
It's ever so good
We have snow fights
And we have good fun
We even build snowmen
But then the sun comes
And it melts the snowman.

Ryan Smith (11)
St John's CE Primary School, Worksop

A Simile Poem

As black as the night in a thunderstorm.
As pink as a baby that has just been born.
As green as leaves growing in the sun.
As red as jam in a round bun.
As gold as a coin in a man's pocket.
As grey as a flying, blasting rocket.

Josh Rose (11)
St John's CE Primary School, Worksop

A Simile Poem

As orange as a fresh orange on a hot day,
As gold as a bright sunset in May.
As yellow as a banana skin on the floor,
As brown as the rocks scattered on the moor.
As black as the sky at night,
As silver as the armour on the knight.

Holly Ashmore (10)
St John's CE Primary School, Worksop

Playground Bullies

Playground bullies stand and glare
Their devilish eyes glow upon my face
Why do they gulp and stare?
This isn't my favourite place

A new kid comes and asks to play
The bullies have caught his eye
I'm pretty sure he'll go away
And I promise I don't lie

My teacher asks, 'What is the matter with this school?'
I point him to the bullies' den
I am a total and utter fool
I'll never be the same again.

Courtney Jones (11)
St John's CE Primary School, Worksop

The White Witch

The witch is very bad and sly,
Tall and thin and really foolish,
The golden wand is very straight,
The witch's face is very white.

The witch likes the animals' fur,
Standing proud and very tall,
She wears a big golden crown,
She has a servant, it is a dwarf.

The witch has a magic wand
That turns people into stone
She always wears a golden crown
She has got blood-red lips.

Samantha Gilfillan (11)
St John's CE Primary School, Worksop

Park Fun

Run through the gate
Climb on the frame
Rush down the slide
Playing my game

Jump through the hoop
Hide in the trees
Chasing by the pond
Falling on my knees

Swing with the swings
Sway with the grass
Sing with flowers
Watch birds pass

Swim in the water
Bathe in the sun
Sit in the shade
Think of what you've done.

Lauren Flower (11)
St John's CE Primary School, Worksop

The Playground

Children kick balls
Toddlers are leaping
Teachers are rapping
Babies are crying

Boys are fighting
Girls are skipping
Helpers are skating
Head teachers are jogging

Nippers are climbing
Teenagers are talking
Pupils are learning
Girls and boys are playing.

Holly Keogh (10)
St John's CE Primary School, Worksop

Colours

Blue as the sparkly, wavy sea,
Red as blood and is always in me.
Green as the grass on a huge field,
Silver as a hard, mighty, great shield.
Yellow as the burning red-hot sun,
Pink as icing on top of a bun.

Black as a big, dark, scary hole,
Brown as muck, homemade for a mole.
Purple as beautiful, shiny leather,
Orange as a long, stretchy tape measure.
Gold as a shiny precious ring,
Bronze as a bell going ring-a-ding-ding.

Darryl Bell (11)
St John's CE Primary School, Worksop

Hate

Hate is like a red fire,
Crackling in the fireplace.
It makes you feel like you are going
To explode with hatred and anger.
It tastes like foul medicine
Sitting in the cupboard.
It smells like smoke
Drifting from the chimney pot.
It looks like a thunderbolt
Flashing through the sky.
It sounds like a train
Huffing down the track.
It reminds me of a big dog
Growling, ready to jump and tear
A little mouse apart like a black panther.

Adriana Perucca (9)
St Mary's Catholic Primary School, Daventry

Excitement

Excitement is yellow like smiley faces
It reminds me of summer when flowers grow
It looks like people having fun at the beach
It feels like something tingling like a star
It tastes like chocolate pudding waiting to be eaten
It smells like a Sunday roast coming out the oven
It sounds like children laughing and giggling at school
It makes me jump for joy.

Dionne Kennedy (9)
St Mary's Catholic Primary School, Daventry

Tiger

Here comes a tiger, short and stout,
He's coming so fast, you hear me shout,
He launches himself at me,
I move away and hit a tree.

Crash, bang, wallop,
Timber!

Josh Steel (11)
St Mary's Catholic Primary School, Daventry

The Croc

There once was a croc from the sea,
Who glided through water swiftly,
He destroyed a small boat
And choked on a fur coat,
So he never got to eat me.

Alexander Crowe (10)
St Mary's Catholic Primary School, Daventry

Hey Little Monkey

Hey little monkey, look at me,
You're such a sweet chimpanzee.
You can do what you want any day,
But may not always get your way.
Your coat is a colour of pinky-brown,
Oh look at that, what a lovely frown.
I bet you like your smelly bath,
I hope I don't get in the way of your nice path.
You walk on your hands and feet,
Which is really pretty neat.
As you eat your lovely bugs,
You give your children lots of hugs.
I wish I was a chimpanzee
Like you and we would walk swiftly.

Sophie Byrne (11)
St Mary's Catholic Primary School, Daventry

At The Zoo

At the monkeys, they are eating bananas,
Ohh, ohh, ahh, ahh.

Here are the lions, the kings of the jungle,
Roar!

There are the seals swimming about,
Arf, arf, splash!

Look at the rattlesnake shaking its tail,
Rattle, rattle, rattle!

Last are the crocodiles lazing about,
Chomp, chomp, yawn!

Alexander Hammond (10)
St Mary's Catholic Primary School, Daventry

Kangaroo Kennings

High jumper
Baby carrier
Joey grower
Everyday eaters
Everyday drinkers
Outback liver
Jumping joeys.

Collette Musgrove (9)
St Mary's Catholic Primary School, Daventry

My Bike Ride

I ride on my bike in a hurry to get home,
I go down the street and ride over a stone,
I got up and rode my bike down the road,
I go to my friend's flat but her door had a new code,
So I go home in hunger for some tea,
I get home, 'What's happened to your knee?'

Mollie Phipps (10)
St Mary's Catholic Primary School, Daventry

Happiness

Happiness is multicoloured like fireworks exploding,
It sounds like waves crashing against the rocks,
It smells like fish and chips,
It tastes like melting chocolate,
It feels like laughter
And reminds me of when I play.

Megan Coy (9)
St Mary's Catholic Primary School, Daventry

Fear

Fear is pale blue like an ocean of water,
It feels like a tsunami smashing against your body,
It tastes like an ocean being dropped into your mouth,
It smells like sweat pouring out of your body,
It sounds like a million rats coming to attack you,
It looks like a person turning into stone,
It reminds me of a car crash, all the noises going round my head.

Saoirse Welland (9)
St Mary's Catholic Primary School, Daventry

Crocodile Sock

I went to the outback one day
And wandered far, far away,
I met a *big* croc,
Who was wearing a sock,
I paid him some money,
Cos I thought it was funny,
But he bit my head off with shock.

Ben Jalland (9)
St Mary's Catholic Primary School, Daventry

Camel

Have you ever seen an animal
With a lump on its back
Which goes through the desert
Just like that?

George Duffy (10)
St Mary's Catholic Primary School, Daventry

In The Playground

The bell! It's playtime!
Struggling into jackets,
Lining up, making plans
For fun and games.

Children running,
Children talking,
Skipping, jumping,
Chasing, yelling.

The bell! Playtime is over.
Struggling out of jackets,
Lining up, back to class,
Back to work.

Natasha Kimber (9)
St Peter's RC Primary School, Aberdeen

It's Playtime

The bell! It's playtime!
Pencils down, it's time to line up.
I'm getting excited.
Planning our games.
I can't wait to get out.

Bursting out of the school door,
Like bees buzzing out of a hive.
Running this way and that,
Jumping, skipping and hopping.

The bell! Playtime is over.
Time to line up.
Marching back inside,
Like an army of ants.

Paul Angus (8)
St Peter's RC Primary School, Aberdeen

It's Playtime

The bell! It's playtime, I love playtime!
In the playground I see children
Skipping and running, jumping and laughing.

Girls are screaming, boys are shouting,
The traffic on the road is noisy,
But it can't beat us!

There goes the bell!
Almost time to get in line.
Almost time to get back to work.

Farai Nyadundu (8)
St Peter's RC Primary School, Aberdeen

War

War is all around me,
All around my dead family's bodies,
War is all around me.

War is hurting me,
Hurting me inside, mentally,
War is hurting me.

War is hurting others,
Hurting others as they are at the air raid shelters,
Knowing they'll be next,
War is hurting others.

War is killing,
Killing innocent lives,
War is killing.

War is destroying,
Destroying people, homes,
War is destroying.

But what can I do to prevent it?
Nothing!
I have to grin and bear it!

Mischa Macpherson (11)
Sandwickhill School, Isle of Lewis

War Time

I hear the air raid siren ringing,
We all start rushing to the shelter,
To a place where we will be safe.

I hear the German planes,
Flying over our heads,
Dropping bombs on their way.

I quickly open the door
To see what's there,
I see the spotlights in the sky,
Searching for planes.
I see soldiers rushing everywhere,
To make sure that we're all safe.

I feel scared,
That I'm going to die,
But as I sit with my family,
I feel happy.

John Macaulay (11)
Sandwickhill School, Isle of Lewis

The Tiger's Revenge

The tiger roams the mountains,
The tiger wants his mate,
The tiger sniffs the air and then,
Knows she isn't just late.

The tiger keeps on searching,
He must not lose his head,
He searches though it is no use,
He knows his mate is dead.

The tiger must keep looking,
For the poachers that came this way,
Maybe he won't catch them for years,
But he knows he'll get revenge one day.

Helen Low (10)
Sandwickhill School, Isle of Lewis

The Destruction Of War

The crash of bombs
could be heard outside.
The sun had gone
behind a cloud.
Everything was dark
apart from a shining light
coming from
tent number 1.

Down at tent number 1,
jolly soldiers were singing
about going home.
Suddenly a plane
flew overhead,
saw the light,
dropped a bomb.

All 56 men and
more died.

Mairi Maclean (11)
Sandwickhill School, Isle of Lewis

War And Peace

W ar and peace
A re very different
R eally, I think so

A peaceful place can be
N ear a big war
D id you know that?

P eace is what I want the most
E xcept I can't have it
A war is going on
C ome and see
E verywhere around you.

Louise Campbell (11)
Sandwickhill School, Isle of Lewis

Seasons

We walk along the road and see the daffodils.
We also see the lambs around us.
It's springtime!

While we play on beaches
The sun shines all around us.
We see the butterflies fly beside us.
Flowers bloom. We have great fun.
It's summertime!

Leaves fall off trees,
We can have great fun,
Run and jump in the leaves,
It's autumn time!

Snow starts to fall,
We put up our Christmas tree.
On Christmas Day we open our presents.
It's wintertime!

Gillian Johnson (10)
Sandwickhill School, Isle of Lewis

I Hate War

It's war again
Death is everywhere,
Armies sent away
To fight for victory.

Disease is spreading
Faster than sadness,
Everyone carries a gun
Just in case.

Planes fly past
To drop the bombs,
Everyone runs for cover,
Hopefully we'll survive.

Holly MacIver (11)
Sandwickhill School, Isle of Lewis

War Is Horrible

War is horrible, it's no fun,
It breaks up families
And it brings out the worst in people.
People you love get hurt,
Men die for their country,
War brings out sadness.
Fathers leave home,
Mothers have to work,
One bomb can bring out a whole village.
So many people die
Because of one man.

Seona Scott (12)
Sandwickhill School, Isle of Lewis

Scotland

S cotland has history everywhere you go.
C astles here and there, some are quite a sight.
O ver the hills and over the sea,
T owns, cities, places to your delight.
L oads of nature walks, parks to see,
A ctivities for young and old.
N ever bored in Scotland, things to do from
D own in the Borders to up in Highlands.

Mhairi Shaw (11)
Sandwickhill School, Isle of Lewis

Siege

S o many people dying.
I hope I don't get shot by an arrow.
E veryone is fighting.
G osh, I've just been hit by an arrow.
E verything is turning into a blur.

Ian Maciver (11)
Sandwickhill School, Isle of Lewis

Cycling

C ool, soft breeze as I go downhill.
Y oung, cold, I feel free!
C linging onto the handlebars.
L ooking down, get my steering right.
I nside my body my heart is racing.
N ight draws near, oh dear!
G oing in now, the atmosphere was *great!*

Ailidh Macleay (10)
Sandwickhill School, Isle of Lewis

My Dog, Gary

M y dog, Gary, is an old dog
Y ou really would like him, if you met him

D ogs can sometimes be clever, but Gary is silly
O ld dogs usually can't run so well, but Gary is a good runner
G ary is a good, loving and very nice dog

G ood as gold he is
A really pretty dog, I love him very much
R eally, I don't want him to die
Y ou are the best dog in the world, Gary!

Amy Fraser (10)
Sandwickhill School, Isle of Lewis

Vehicles

V ery fast these vehicles are,
E very mile is very far.
H ow fast do these go?
I njections, turbos, they don't go slow,
C ars are cool, so are bikes,
L ots more fun than little trikes.
E very mile these things go.
S low! What do you mean slow?

Liam Ferguson (10)
Sandwickhill School, Isle of Lewis

Football Crazy

Football, got to play football,
Now,
I can't wait,
Please play football
Or I'll have to go and skate.

We can play lots of games,
Heads and volleys, come and play.

Now it's time to go,
No more football until tomorrow.

Football crazy,
Football mad,
Thanks for helping,
I'm so glad.

Ryan Maclean (10)
Sandwickhill School, Isle of Lewis

We Love Pets

W onderful,
E xciting,

L oved all over,
O ld and young but always special,
V ery nice,
E asy to look after,

P erfect to play with,
E xtraordinary,
T oo brilliant to explain.
S o special to everyone.

Jessie Lyness (10)
Sandwickhill School, Isle of Lewis

A Winter Dream Poem

Winter's air,
Winds blow,
Icy rivers,
With a blanket of snow.

Chimney's smoke,
Cars cold,
Piled snow,
While Jack Frost rolls.

The air is cold,
Noses red,
The ice I hold,
As I dream in bed.

Latham Russell (9)
Stanton-under-Bardon Primary School, Markfield

Winter's Day

Snow falling,
People snoring,
Winter's morning,
How appalling,

Cars moving,
Kids pleasing,
Adults sneezing,

Houses white,
All so bright,
Snowballs flying,
Babies crying.

Stefan Barrett (9)
Stanton-under-Bardon Primary School, Markfield

Christmas Day

C hristmas crackers, crackling and crunching,
H appy feelings all day long.
R udolph rampaging round Rotherham, like a starving fox
chasing a terrified turkey.
I n every house, every room, people playing like baboons,
S ledging along slippery surfaces, screaming, shouting in the snow,
T angled tinsel in the tall tree,
M emories from years before, bring many moments of joy,
A rrangements made, people arriving,
S anta swooping overhead, like a jumbo jet without any fuel.

Joe Parr (9)
Stanton-under-Bardon Primary School, Markfield

My Brother

My brother is the rage in heartburn,
My brother is the explosion in a bomb,
My brother is the agony when you're bitten by an insect,
My brother is full of energy that never runs out,
My brother is a fly buzzing around your head,
My brother is the taste of a Galaxy chocolate bar.

Samuel Clements (9)
Stanton-under-Bardon Primary School, Markfield

My Brother

My brother is the horrible pain of the burning cuts on my knees.
My brother is a boring chatterbox who never shuts up.
My brother is so noisy you can hear him anywhere on Earth.
My brother is a pig, snorting in a squishy, squashy river.
My brother is an impassionate little wimp.
My brother is the beat of love inside my heart.

Bethany Southam (10)
Stanton-under-Bardon Primary School, Markfield

Child Of The Week

Monday's child wakes up early and moans
As she miserably mopes down the stairs for her breakfast.
Tuesday's child has her tasty tomato soup
Before brushing her twinkling teeth.
Wednesday's child wants her wish to come true,
About searching for dolphins in the ocean.
Thursday's child thinks she's the third person
To thank her friend for thumping the bully.
Friday's child is happy because she is free
From school for two whole days.
Saturday's child goes swimming, goes to the shop,
Gets some Smarties and slopes in front of the television
Stuffing herself with sweets.
But the child born on the Sabbath Day is kind,
Thoughtful and loves to play.

Kate Davies (9)
Stanton-under-Bardon Primary School, Markfield

My Brother

My brother is the howl of a gust of wind,
Racing and squeezing through the middle of my ear.
My brother is the pain of an electric shock
That just zapped me with pain.
My brother is so noisy you could hear him from Mars
With earmuffs on.
My brother is like a twirling, twisting, crashing tornado,
Just waiting to blow you away.
My brother is like a deadly and fearsome tidal wave,
Ready to wash you away with a single splash.
But sometimes he can be a beat of love, inside your heart.

William Preston (10)
Stanton-under-Bardon Primary School, Markfield

Things You Find In A Goblin's Pocket

A shiny pot of gold,
A raw half-eaten fish,
A mouldy eye,
A bloody dagger,
A black and white crow,
A dead soft pumpkin,
A human's head,
A wizard's wand,
A dead frog,
Quicksand in a jar,
Some human guts all pink,
A scaly dragon,
Green mouldy mushrooms,
A teacher's brown long wig,
A troll's wooden club,
A black spider,
500 worms
And me, *help!*

Kyle Andrews (11)
Stockton Heath Primary School, Warrington

End Of School Desk Clear-Out

A mouldy sandwich and some cheese,
My very old house keys.
Ten snapped pencils I'd never used,
Some laces I nicked from my friend's shoes.
A piece of sticky gum,
A very hard sum.
A book I never read,
My best friend's ted.
My stuffed pet rat,
Who was run over and now flat.
A mix of anxiety, excitement and doubt,
That's all I found at the end of school desk clear-out!

Lindsey Campbell (10)
Stockton Heath Primary School, Warrington

Who Am I? Kennings

Secret hider,
Gadget seeker,
Detective finder,
Nosy peeker,
Scary looker,
Silent talker,
Good follower,
Crime solver
And wall crawler
Who am I?

Rohan Shukla (10)
Stockton Heath Primary School, Warrington

Hobbit Kennings

Hole dweller
Story teller
Plant buyer
Bacon fryer
Pipe smoker
Cheery joker
Ale drinker
Deep thinker.

Jen George (11)
Stockton Heath Primary School, Warrington

Horses

Fast racer
Grass grazer
Friend lover
Apple eater
Super speeder.

Abigail Taylor (10)
Stockton Heath Primary School, Warrington

Executioner Kennings

Head slicer
Throat slitter
Blood spurter
Flesh thrower
Soul eater
Organ picker
Body hider
Gore shredder
Bone breaker
Sword sharpener
Axe swinger
Human killer!

Daniel Robinson (10)
Stockton Heath Primary School, Warrington

The Queen Who Ate A Chilli Bean

There was a Spanish queen
Who ate a chilli bean
Her face went red
And as for her head
It blew up so it couldn't be seen!

Molly Hughes (11)
Stockton Heath Primary School, Warrington

Rain Haiku

The pitter-patter
of raindrops landing softly
against the rooftops.

Erin Shepherd (11)
Stockton Heath Primary School, Warrington

Monkey Business Kennings

Nit picker,
Nut flicker,
Banana peeler,
Orange squeezer.

Stunt darer,
Belly barer,
Vine swinger,
Tree climber.

Canopy singer,
Mother clinger,
Milk giver,
Berry pincher.

Thomas Mooney (11)
Stockton Heath Primary School, Warrington

A Horse Kennings

Field walker,
Carrot chewer,
Owner stalker,
Ride giver,
Apple eater,
Gorgeous creature,
Mischievous peeper,
Fun carer,
Attention seeker,
Fast racer,
Hay eater,
Loving creature.

Charlotte Johnson (10)
Stockton Heath Primary School, Warrington

Guess Who? Kennings

Tree hugger
Bush hider
Leaf scoffer
Branch clinger
Tree hogger
Daytime snoozer
Sun lover
Daily cleaner
Lazy bather
Night-time relaxer
Baby cuddler

Who am I?

Melissa Cliffe (10)
Stockton Heath Primary School, Warrington

Autumn

Autumn rain splashes,
Wind stirs fiery leaves away,
Across the woodland.

Small mammals scurry,
The winter cold approaches -
Frost is on the way.

Icy fingers reach,
Clasping the path, the forest,
Cold chills the night air.

Mist engulfs the dawn,
Searching hawk swoops, a new day,
Silent village sleeps.

Claire Boreham (10)
Stockton Heath Primary School, Warrington

Shall We Go To Huxter?

Shall we go to Huxter and see
Joan's sheep jumping together in the field
In front of the house like Jack jumping on the bed?

Stuart's new house blocking out the sun
Like a giant mountain?

Shall we go to Huxter and hear
Edward's rusty old quad engine start
In the garage chugging and puffing?

Seagulls and sparrows fighting for a place on the bird table,
Like me and Jack fighting over a toy?

Shall we go to Huxter and smell
Granny's coal fire burning away, with black, choking smoke?
Oh! and I see a seagull flying into the smoke,
Farewell bird, I knew thee well.

Mum's cheesy pasta cooking in the oven,
With a cheesy smell like melting cheese on a pizza.

Rhys Hughson (11)
Whalsay School, Whalsay

Volcano

Volcanoes are high, brown
About to erupt.
Volcanoes are hot, extremely hot,
Volcanoes are bubbly.

Mountains are high,
With a white tip.
Mountains are cold, very cold.

My house is white,
With an orange roof.
My house has hens to the left.
My house has me.

Holly Jamieson (10)
Whalsay School, Whalsay

Strange

To see a cat eat a rat, is a normal sight,
But a *rat* that eats a *cat* is just not right.
I've seen a mouse that lives in a house,
But not a house that lives in a mouse.

I've heard of a barking dog,
But never heard of a barking bog.
It sounds like a strange sight,
But if you think about it, it could be right.

I've seen a bat with flying wings,
But haven't heard a hat that sings.
Fish live in the sea that's very salty,
If they were mechanical, they would be faulty.

I've heard of an electric eel,
But never an electric seal.
It might not sound right to you,
But if you think about it, it could be true.

Stewart Hutchison (11)
Whalsay School, Whalsay

Shall We Go To Isbister?

Shall we go to Isbister and watch and listen
To the birds chirping and flying away from the dog's barking?

Dogs chasing after one another and barking at the sheep in the park.

I can hear sheep baaing and crunching on the grass in the park.

I watch cars zooming past Woodstock.

I can hear the gate being opened by Neil with his bike.

Listen to the tractors whirring, dogs barking
And the sheep baaing from in by.

And as the sun sets over the hills, watch all the lights
Come on in bonnie peerie Isbister.

Sarah Polson (11)
Whalsay School, Whalsay

Weather

Here
The weather is not very nice.
The rain
Pours down
Day after day.
There is hardly a day
Without wind.

The temperature
Hardly gets
Above 10 degrees.
Neither
Do we have much sun,
But that doesn't mean
You
Can't have fun!

Greg Anderson (10)
Whalsay School, Whalsay

My Senses Poem

Listen to the fiddlers playing their fiddles,
Playing high and playing low notes and different songs.

Touch silver, shiny metal sitting on a bench.

Listen to the wind blowing all over the place,
Blowing over toys outside.

See an old woman slowly walking down the street,
Crossing the road with cars zooming by.

See bigger houses than Buckingham Palace.

Taste pepperoni pizza with pepperoni on top.

Smell oil out of a quad.

A piece of rotten wood.

James Shearer (11)
Whalsay School, Whalsay

A Cat In A Hat

I once had a cat
Who wore a hat,
He lived in my house
And caught a mouse.

He came from Spain
And had such a pain from yesterday,
When he caught that mouse
In my house.

My cat sat by the fire,
While Mum got rid of that mouse,
In my house.

The mouse stole the cat's hat
And ran flat
Out of the house

And that was the end
Of the mouse
In my house.

Alice Pottinger (10)
Whalsay School, Whalsay

Shall We Go To Sandwick?

Shall we go to Sandwick
And hear the cats miaowing from the warm garage?
You can see the flowers glowing brightly in the dark.
You can smell the black smoke from a fire on a rocky beach.
You can hear the fast wind whistling through the creaky,
twirly clothes line.
You can see the woolly sheep lying exhausted on the rough grass.
You can smell Uncle Maurice's rotten compost bin.

Bryan Hutchison (12)
Whalsay School, Whalsay

Horses

Horses running through the field,
Lots of different colours;
Orange, black, white and brown.

Horses need lots of attention,
When you ride them,
Beware!
You may get a little scare.

If you love them,
They'll love you.
Take good care of horses,
Because if you don't,
They may get ill.

Horses need fresh water every day
And lots of grass to chew.
If you don't give them what they want,
You could end up
With a very moody horse.

Valerie Sales (10)
Whalsay School, Whalsay

Shall We Go To North Park?

Shall we go to North Park
To hear the lambs baaing in the fields,
The waves roaring and crashing,
The seagulls squawking in the wind.
I can see the pier with boats going in and out,
On the horizon I can sometimes see
The distant sails of yachts
Or a pinky, orange sunset.
The men taking in the lobster creels
Or tending the salmon farm.
You can hear the sleet on the windows
And feel the steel wind on your face in winter.

Conor Cosnett (11)
Whalsay School, Whalsay

My Senses Poem

Listen to the noise of my rabbits scratch the cage
I can hear the noise of a bumble bee
Listen to the birds sitting in the tree
I can hear my first cousin Gary, going up the road on his motorbike.

I can touch a feather fallen from a bird,
Or feel Gary's motorbike all hot, because it's just been used
I can touch the grass that has been rained on
And feel a really prickly cactus.

You can look at the animals in the zoo
See the sunshine on the hill
See the amazing car on the road
See the shadows of the tree.

Taste Thelma's stewed sausages, mmm
Taste a yummy chip
I can taste a melted Mars bar, mmm
Taste a very yummy cream cake.

Smell the petrol out of the quad
Smell the deodorant fresh from the shop
Smell garlic just being cooked
Smell the perfume of a woman.

Steven Thompson (11)
Whalsay School, Whalsay

Shall We Go To Isbister?

Shall we go to Isbister
And hear the sheep eating the grass?
I can hear Jimmy caaing his little lambs.
Smell the little flower in the garden.
I can see the Filla crashing through the waves.
See Dad fixing his rusty pick-up in the garage.
Listen to the birds singing in the tree.
See Vanna in our house scratching the green mat.
Look at Laureen's old roof
And Robbie's old rusty tractor.

Magnus Eunson (11)
Whalsay School, Whalsay

Shall We Go To North Park?

Shall we go to North Park,
Go and hear
Lots of vehicles passing by
And hear a boat coming in to the pier?

Shall we go to North Park
And see sheep eyes
Glistening in the dark
And see a boat going by?

Shall we go to North Park
And smell
The sheep in the park
And smell the petrol
Of my quad?

Steve Pottinger (12)
Whalsay School, Whalsay

My Senses Poem

Listen to the cats miaowing in the shed
Stuck in a creel
Hear the two cats fighting in the garage

Feel the smooth cat hair on its body

See cats fighting in the house
See a pretty sunset

Taste some melons sitting on the table

Smell the cat's cat food, poof, disgusting!
Smell my pizza in the oven, lovely!

Cheryl Arthur (11)
Whalsay School, Whalsay

An Animal's Advice

Mole
I like my home
Please don't destroy it
Your footsteps are like thunder
Trampling over my home

Pig
I like my looks
Also my skin
Don't turn me into bacon
Nice and thick
Feed me well
Or I'll become a stick

Owl
I like my feathers
Nice and thick
Listen to me shriek and hoot
In the thick, calm night

Budgie
I'm a budgie, I twitter and squawk
But you might as well give up Buster
You can't make me talk
Being crammed up in this cage
Is not very cool
And I hate that jumper you wear
Made out of wool.

Tom Hutchison (11)
Whalsay School, Whalsay

My Senses Poem

Hear
Hear the birds singing to and fro
Listen to the trees moving back and forth
Listen to the cars rushing past
Hear the motorbikes roaring past

Smell
Can you smell the sweet countryside as we go by?
Can you smell the petrol coming from a car?
Can you smell the horrible scent of rabbit litter?
Can you smell the sweet smell of apple shampoo?

Feel
Can you feel the soft fur from a rabbit?
Can you feel the wire on the hens' cage?
Can you feel the table round and flat?
Can you feel the cactus sharp and sore?

See
Can you see the rabbits running around?
Can you see a crab running around on the bottom?
Can you see an aeroplane up in the sky?
Can you see the animals in the zoo getting fed?

Taste
Can you taste a hot cheese pizza?
Can you taste a melted Mars bar?
Can you taste a chocolate cake?
Can you taste a bit of mint ice cream very cold?

Abbey Irvine (11)
Whalsay School, Whalsay

Animal Thoughts

Mountain Pony
Please don't capture me and sell me.
I want to live my life as you want to live yours.
If you are kind enough,
Leave some old peelings to the herd.
Thank you.

Iguana
Just leave me be, don't handle me.
I know you like to touch my scaly body,
But just leave me alone.
You just love to have exotic pets,
But we hate to be kept in a cage,
Leave me be!

Fox
Oh no, it's the hunting season again,
Dogs sniffing me out.
Horses' hooves stamping on the ground,
Leave me alone,
My life is a misery.
I like to snuggle up in my little den,
But one day I hear sawing and cutting,
Loud noises, I want my life to be quiet!

Tiger
Leave my fur alone, it may look good on you,
But leave it where it is please.
My homeland is important to me,
Don't mess with it,
Chopping down trees, chainsaws blaring,
I want peace and quiet.

Lynda Hutchison (12)
Whalsay School, Whalsay

My Senses Poem

Hear
The bird chirping in the trees
The horns on cars going beep, beep
The phone ringing in the classroom
The doors slamming in the wind
The bagpipes playing at festivals

Touch
My teeth hard and smooth
A cactus all prickly and rough
A seal smooth and wet
A banana all slimy and gooey
My hair soft and shiny

See
A rabbit all furry and cute
Boats so big and strong
An oar going really fast
The aeroplane zooming through the sky
The trees waving in the wind

Taste
Ice cream cold in my mouth
Crisps all crumbling in your mouth
Cakes so sweet and nice
A Mars bar chocolaty and sweet
Pancakes hot with syrup

Smell
Petrol strong and smelly
Feet very smelly and horrible
Shampoo smells very nice
Rabbit litter stinks very badly
Garlic, a very strong smell.

Megan Jamieson (12)
Whalsay School, Whalsay

Senses

Listen to the wind battling against the gate
Hear the rain hammering against the window
Listen to the waves crashing against the rocks
Hear the muffled voices at the end of the corridor

Touch a smooth, hard table
Or soft feathers
Feel the rough bark of a tree
Touch silky soft velvet

Taste a sour lemon
Eat some thick creamy yoghurt
Or a sweet strawberry
Taste sweet golden syrup slipping down your tongue

See trees waving their branches
Watch a sun setting on a hill
Watch white clouds all different shapes and sizes
See flowers blooming bright in different colours

A smell of fish straight from the sea
Smell petrol straight from a car
Smell shampoo, fruity and organic
Smell popcorn with syrup on top.

Tammi Anderson (11)
Whalsay School, Whalsay

Colours

Red
Is the colour of blood,
Dripping down my knee,
For some reason,
I let no others see.

Green
Is like the grass growing,
Really fast.

Blue
is the sea,
Calm and settled,
As can be.

Gold
Is fame and fortune,
Rather made for me.

Silver
Pennies shining in the sun,
It is the colour of the 'golden' gun.

Bronze,
The medal I always win
Or that forgotten tin
That Mother threw in the bin.

White
Clouds high up in the sky.
It's where I'll go
When I die.

Andy Williamson (10)
Whalsay School, Whalsay

Shall We Go To Skibberhoull?

Shall we go to Skibberhoull and hear the birds chirping?
You can't see them as they have gone back to their nests.

Shall we go to Skibberhoull to see the sheep being chased by a dog?

Shall we go to Skibberhoull to smell Allister's byre
Where his cows live?

Shall we go to Skibberhoull to smell my granny's flowers
Swaying in the breeze?

Shall we go to Skibberhoull to hear vehicles pass by,
Like a rocket in outer space?

Shall we go to Skibberhoull and see a boat pass by
Over the horizon but I can't tell what boat it is?

Shall we go to Skibberhoull and hear my granny sing along
To the radio (and badly at that)?

Shall we go to Skibberhoull and see nature all around?
There's Mr Rabbit over there in the corner and there's Mrs Hedgehog,
Who I nearly stood on, (I don't think she was very pleased).

Shall we go to Skibberhoull and hear people working with hard,
Smelly wood and people working with engines?

John Irvine (11)
Whalsay School, Whalsay

Senses

Listen to the birds singing in the spring breeze
The sea waves crash on the shore
See the bees make nectar to honey
The flowers sway in the breeze

Smell the garlic, they make my eyes cry
Smell the countryside, a nice smell indeed
Touch the dogs, some rough, some soft
The ears, soft and cosy

Taste the lamb chops, they're really juicy
The macaroni that's really cheesy
Taste bacon, to me the fat tastes horrid
The cake, I like them, they're creamy

Listen to the piglets squeal for some food
The lambs baa for their ewes
See the lambs hop up and down in the field
The pizza eaten by others and not you

Touch the sheep, woolly and soft
Smell the coffee, what a strong scent
Listen to the bees buzz in the wind
See the crabs scurrying across the beach for food.

George Irvine (11)
Whalsay School, Whalsay

The Great Twinkling World

I travelled into space and guess what I saw?
I saw a planet that had never been discovered.

The beautiful waterfall is as bright as the summer sky at midday.

The long steps are as red as a ruby in a beautiful bubble.

The fairies are as beautiful as a flower from the summer field.

Jessica Benbow (8)
Woodcocks' Well CE Primary School, Stoke-on-Trent

A World Of Make-Believe

I travelled into space and guess what I saw?
I saw a planet that had been discovered before.
The mansion stands still like a tree in a crystal village.
The river is as blue as a diamond.
The moon is as fluffy as a ball of cotton.
The trees smell like chocolate.
The tower shines like a shooting star.
I will never forget that night.

Katie Barlow (8)
Woodcocks' Well CE Primary School, Stoke-on-Trent

Imaginary World

In Imaginary World . . .
The river is as dark as chocolate,
As it swishes through the rocky valley.
The walls are like rainbows
As their magical colours shine.
The palace is as tall as a mountain
Smelling like banana milkshake.
The twisting steps are like tornadoes spinning.
The bridge is as white as a dove
Peacefully swooping side to side.

Megan Oliver (9)
Woodcocks' Well CE Primary School, Stoke-on-Trent

Dreamworld

The waterfall is as beautiful as a blue diamond thundering down.
The doves are like jewels flying through the air.
The steps are red rubies leading to the chocolate river.
The palace is as bright and glittery as a disco ball.

Abbie Rogers (9)
Woodcocks' Well CE Primary School, Stoke-on-Trent

Atlantis

Atlantis is a funny place,
Things are rather weird,
Because . . .
The sky is the ocean on a summer day.
The river is like crystal, shimmering in the light.
Steps are twisted glass that look like they're being drained.
The mountains are as magic as a wizard's room.
Flowers are like jewels, smelling sweet like milky chocolate.
Origami birds are flying lightly like ballet dancers.

Victoria O'Hara (8)
Woodcocks' Well CE Primary School, Stoke-on-Trent

Imaginary World

In Imaginary World . . .
Flowers smell like toffee treats.
Palaces twinkle like shooting stars.
The grass is as blue as the sky.
The trees are like green emeralds.
The roofs of houses sparkle like shimmering pearls.
Shops look like small diamonds.

Georgia Vacquier-Gould (8)
Woodcocks' Well CE Primary School, Stoke-on-Trent

Dreamworld

The sky is like black paint filling the air.
The steep steps twist like a tornado spinning faster every second.
The walls are like colourful rainbows standing side by side.
The river is as clear as crystal flowing down the valley.

Brad Jackson (9)
Woodcocks' Well CE Primary School, Stoke-on-Trent